nly

THE BILLY PLAYS

By the same author

REMEMBRANCE

TIES OF BLOOD

THE BILLY PLAYS

GRAHAM REID

ff

faber and faber

LONDON · BOSTON

First published in 1984 as
Billy: Three Plays for Television by
Faber and Faber Limited
This new edition including *Lorna*
first published in 1987 by
Faber and Faber Limited
3 Queen Square London WC1N 3AU

Filmset by Wilmaset Birkenhead Wirral
Printed in Great Britain by
Redwood Burn Ltd, Trowbridge, Wiltshire

British Library Cataloguing in Publication Data

Reid, J. Graham
The Billy plays. — 2nd ed.
I. Title II. Reid, J. Graham. Billy
822'.914 PR6068.E43/
ISBN 0-571-14725-9

For my wife Irene with love

CONTENTS

TOO LATE TO TALK TO BILLY

Characters

The Martin family:
NORMAN: father
JANET: mother
BILLY: aged 18
LORNA: aged 17
ANN: aged 13
MAUREEN: aged 9

IAN: BILLY's friend
SHIRLEY: IAN's girlfriend
JUNE BOYD: BILLY's girlfriend
MRS BOYD: JUNE's widowed mother
JOHN FLETCHER: a local tough
STEVIE: JANET's ex-lover
NURSES

All three plays are set mainly in West Belfast, during the late seventies.

Too Late to Talk to Billy was first shown on BBC Television on 16 February 1982. The cast was as follows:

NORMAN	James Ellis
BILLY	Kenneth Branagh
LORNA	Brid Brennan
ANN	Tracey Lynch
MAUREEN	Aine Gorman
JANET	Maggie Shevlin
STEVIE	Walter McMonagle
IAN	Colum Convey
SHIRLEY	Chrissie Cotterill
MRS BOYD	Catherine Gibson
JUNE BOYD	Mary Jackson
JOHN FLETCHER	John Hewitt
Producers	Neil Zeiger and Chris Parr
Director	Paul Seed
Designer	Diane Menaul

1. EXT. STREET CORNER. DAY

The corner of a street of small, two-up, two-down houses in the Donegall Road area of Belfast. There is a shop on the corner. IAN *is standing, dressed in combat jacket and peaked denim cap. He has a stripe on his arm, new. He holds two pick-axe handles.* JOHN FLETCHER *arrives, dressed likewise, but with three stripes.*

IAN: Right, John?

JOHN: It's sergeant on duty.

IAN: Oh aye, sorry . . . sergeant.

JOHN: Remember what that stripe means . . . you've an example to show.

(IAN *hands him one of the pick-axe handles.*)

Rank means responsibilities, d'you read me?

IAN: Yes, sergeant.

JOHN: Right . . . let's go.

(*They set off up the road. There should be a long view of the street that closes in on the exterior of the Martins' house, number 63.*)

2. INT. THE MARTINS' LIVING ROOM. DAY

LORNA *is ironing. There is a pile of finished clothes on the chair. She picks up another garment, glances at herself in the large oval-shaped mirror hanging above the mantelshelf, and then carries on.*

3. INT. SCULLERY. DAY

NORMAN *is shaving, his face lathered. His gear is laid out on the draining board. He is using a small circular mirror, suspended from a nail.*

4. INT. CITY HOSPITAL. DAY

A small waiting-room, off a side-ward. ANN *and* MAUREEN *enter from the side-ward where their mother lies close to death. A* NURSE *follows them and speaks. She takes a tissue from her pocket and wipes tears from* MAUREEN*'s cheeks. The girls leave, hand in hand. The* NURSE *looks back into the side-ward. She turns, her back to the doors, contemplating. She leaves. Zoom in on the doors, as if to pass through.*

5. INT. THE MARTINS' LIVING ROOM. DAY

LORNA *is still ironing.* NORMAN *enters from the scullery, half his face shaven.*

NORMAN: Is that shirt near ready?

LORNA: It'll be ready when you are. You'd need to watch where you're going. The UDA seem to be at it all over today.

NORMAN: To hell with the UDA. So you worry about me now do you? (*Pause.*) Just iron the bloody shirt.

LORNA: Are you going up to the hospital tonight?

NORMAN: I've told you, I've a message to do.

LORNA: Dad . . .

NORMAN: Never mind all that. There's too many people in this house trying to tell me what to do. She doesn't even know me half the time anyway.

LORNA: That's not the point . . .

NORMAN: Point my arse, you know what the point is . . . just smooth the shirt.

(LORNA *and* NORMAN *look at each other for a moment. He breaks away and goes back into the scullery. She finishes the shirt. He returns drying his face with the towel. She gives him the shirt and he starts to put it on.*)

Are my shoes polished?

LORNA: Yes, they're sitting beside your bed.

(*Pause.*)

NORMAN: Are you going up tonight?

LORNA: No. (*Pause.*) No . . .

NORMAN: No, and everything's understood and forgiven because you cry about it.

LORNA: It's not just that . . . I don't like leaving them at night, especially when there's trouble . . . I'll . . . I'll go up tomorrow afternoon. Billy'll maybe go up tonight.

(*He takes a pound from his pocket and places it on the ironing board.*)

NORMAN: Aye, well, maybe he can get her a few grapes or something.

LORNA: She can't eat.

NORMAN: What! Oh aye. Well lemonade or something.

LORNA: Dad . . .

NORMAN: Look . . . I have to go out.

(*Pause.* NORMAN *goes upstairs.* LORNA *puts the pound into her pocket. She starts putting the ironing board down. She puts it into the scullery.* BILLY *enters.*)

LORNA: What's it like on the road?

BILLY: Normal. Roadblocks. Able-bodied men in hiding, the rest in uniform.

LORNA: Will you be all right to go up to the hospital tonight?

BILLY: Is he not going up?

LORNA: He's a message to do.

BILLY: A message! What about the rest of us? I'm supposed to be meeting June at half seven.

LORNA: I'm sorry Billy, I'd go, but . . .

BILLY: No I'm not asking you to go. He should be going . . . him.

LORNA: Could you not wait until half seven and take June with you?

BILLY: No . . . Jasus it's bad enough without having spectators. (*Pause.*) I'll go . . . somebody has to be with her. I'll think of something about June. That lying oul frigger.

LORNA: Say nothing. He left a pound to get her grapes, or lemonade.

BILLY: Why didn't you tell him to stuff his conscience money.

LORNA: Billy, just drop it.

(NORMAN *comes downstairs, dressed in his suit. Combs his hair in the mirror above the mantelshelf.*)

NORMAN: (*To* BILLY) What's it like out?

BILLY: Don't know. I haven't had it out for days.

LORNA: It's quieter, Dad.

NORMAN: (*Pointedly to* BILLY) Is the road still blocked?

BILLY: Why aren't you going up tonight?

NORMAN: I've asked you a question.

BILLY: And I've asked you one.

(NORMAN *and* BILLY *glare at each other.*)

LORNA: Dad might be going up with me tomorrow.

NORMAN: Don't make excuses for me, girl.

BILLY: There is no excuse for you, Da.

NORMAN: Am I accountable to you? (*Pause.*) Am I?

(BILLY *turns away in disgust.*)

Don't you question me, boy. Don't you question where I go, or what I do.

BILLY: (*Swinging round, angrily*) Your wife . . .

LORNA: Billy. . . !

(MAUREEN *enters. She senses the tension.* NORMAN *looks from* BILLY *to her. He is going to speak, but thinks better of it. Pause.*)

Maureen . . . what kept you?

NORMAN: I'm going.

(*He stands for a moment. Nobody speaks. He goes.*)

LORNA: Where's Ann?

MAUREEN: She's down at the corner gossiping.

LORNA: What kept you?

MAUREEN: We were watching the soldiers taking a bus back.

LORNA: That Ann one's no sense. How often have you two been told not to stand watching? When there's trouble you get straight home. That's how children get hurt.

MAUREEN: I didn't get hurt.

BILLY: Don't hang about again. You didn't get hurt this time but you mightn't be so lucky in future. Do you hear me?

LORNA: There's no point getting at the child. It's that Ann one.

6. EXT. STREET CORNER. DAY

ANN *and* TWO SCHOOLFRIENDS *are standing watching as* IAN *is drilling half a dozen local teenage boys.* JOHN FLETCHER *looks on.* NORMAN *approaches.* ANN *sees him and runs home past him.* NORMAN *continues to approach* JOHN FLETCHER *and his troop. He walks straight on, scattering them. We see* JOHN FLETCHER*'s reaction of impotent rage.*

7. INT. THE MARTINS' LIVING ROOM. DAY

ANN *enters.*

BILLY: (*Angrily*) The next time you're out with that child you get her straight home here. How many times have you been told not to stand gaping when there's trouble?

ANN: Oh it was dead funny. The two soldiers took this bus and a wee drunk man came up and tried to give the soldier his fare. All the tyres were flat so then he tried to borra' a wee boy's bike pump. Then another big soldier came over, a cheeky big get, and knocked the wee man's money all over the road. I lifted ten pee.

BILLY: Are you listening to what I'm saying to you?

ANN: It's all right, nobody saw me.

BILLY: I'm telling you not to hang about when there's trouble.

ANN: (*Slightly peeved that* BILLY *is angry with her.*) All right, I heard you. There's no need to write a song about it. Here, if that wee drunk man had been my da, he'd have wrapped that soldier's rifle round his neck for him.

BILLY: The next time somebody might wrap something round your neck, and if they don't I bloody well will.

LORNA: Billy . . . Ann, I want you to go to the chippy. (*Pause.*)

ANN: What do you want?

LORNA: Get two fish suppers and a chip, we'll divide them up.

BILLY: I don't want any.

LORNA: Why not, sure you've had no tea, you'll have to eat something.

BILLY: All right . . .

MAUREEN: Billy, my mummy kept calling me Sarah.

BILLY: Aye, she does that sometimes.

MAUREEN: Why?

BILLY: Well, she sh . . .

LORNA: She just gets confused, Maureen.

MAUREEN: But she could see me, she was awake.

LORNA: I know, but her injections get her all jumbled up.

MAUREEN: Why do they give them to her, if they make her stupid like that?

BILLY: She needs them . . . for the pain.

MAUREEN: I asked her when she was coming home, and she started to cry. Then she said her daddy didn't allow her out. (*Pause.*) Who's Norman, Lorna? She kept on and on about Norman.

BILLY: You know bloody well Norman's my da.

MAUREEN: Oh, that Norman. I've never heard her call him that before.

BILLY: Was she asking why he wasn't up?

MAUREEN: I don't know what she was mumbling about.

ANN: (*In defence of her father*) He sent her up flowers.

BILLY: He must be practising for sending the wreath.

MAUREEN: What wreath?

LORNA: Billy! (*To* MAUREEN) Never you mind.

MAUREEN: She kept going on about . . .

LORNA: All right Maureen, that's enough for now. She didn't know what she was saying. (*Pause.*) Look . . . let's get our tea.

(*She gives the money to* ANN.)

BILLY: Was Ian at the corner, Ann?

ANN: (*Pleased that* BILLY*'s anger at her has gone*) Aye, he's all dressed up in his combat jacket and all, ordering all the wee lads around. John Fletcher's there too, the creep. My da just walked through them all. If a real soldier comes up the road, you won't see them for dust.

BILLY: If Ian's there when you go down, tell him I'd like to see him.

LORNA: Hurry up now, and watch that road.

(ANN *goes.*)

I'll do the tea and butter some bread. Are you taking Ian with you?

BILLY: No I am not. I'll ask him to go up and meet June. I'll call up at her house after.

LORNA: Is that wise, Billy, away up there with all this trouble?

BILLY: Stop fussing will you.

8. EXT. PUBLIC HOUSE. EVENING

NORMAN *approaches and enters the pub.*

9. INT. MARTINS' LIVING ROOM. EVENING

Just after they've eaten. LORNA *is clearing up the plates.*

LORNA: I'll put the kettle on for the dishes, Ann.

ANN: That fish was rotten, it was all batter.

BILLY: You can have him up, for too much a-salt and battery.

ANN: Billy, was that a joke, or are you just trying to talk?

MAUREEN: Lorna, can I go round to Sandra's house to see the film?

LORNA: What time's it over at?

MAUREEN: About ten, I think.

LORNA: Ann can leave you round and then I'll collect you.

ANN: What about the dishes?

LORNA: You'll have them done before you go.

ANN: Am I allowed out?

BILLY: No.

ANN: Stuck in here all the time, I'm sick of it. All the rest are allowed out.

BILLY: You're not, and that's final.

ANN: If my ma was here . . .

LORNA: (*Sharply*) Ann . . . Mum's not here, and you're not going out.

(*Pause.* IAN *raps the door and enters. Still dressed in combat jacket, cap etc.*)

BILLY: In the name of Jasus, what are you supposed to be?

IAN: Jealousy'll get you nowhere, mate. Here, (*offers his arm*) look at that . . . eh?

BILLY: Somebody been chalking on you?

IAN: Chalk! What do you mean chalk? That's a stripe, son, that's sewn on. No oul rubbish here.

ANN: Are you a general now, Ian?

IAN: Close enough, love, close enough.

BILLY: Is the alert over, or are the Martians still expected?

IAN: Eternal vigilantes, that's what Churchill said, and that's what we are.

BILLY: If the army catch you in that outfit they'll bounce you up to Castlereagh on your head.

LORNA: Would you like a cup of tea, Ian?

IAN: No thanks, love, not when I'm on duty. What's wrong, you're not watching 'Doctor Who', Maureen?

MAUREEN: The telly's broke and the man from Gilmore's won't come to fix it 'cause my da owes them money.

LORNA: Maureen, you don't tell your business to everyone.

MAUREEN: I didn't, I just told Ian.

IAN: Look at this stripe, Lorna. An officer and a gentleman now. My lips are sealed.

BILLY: They'd better be, or I'll take that stripe off and sew it across them.

LORNA: How's Shirley, Ian?

IAN: Ah, she's all right. Still can't believe her luck at getting me.

LORNA: You two'll be getting married any day.

IAN: Married! Is your head cut? You'll not catch me getting married.

BILLY: If you start now you could have your own wee army before long.

IAN: Huh, I'd rather fight the next war on me own, than get an army that way. (*Pause.*) What was it you wanted me for?

BILLY: I'm supposed to be meeting June at half seven. But my da can't make it . . . so now I'll have to go up to the hospital and see the old woman.

IAN: You want me to stand in for you, do you? Let her have a real man for one night?

BILLY: Aye, I'm like that. Would you go and meet her and explain? Tell her I'm sorry. It's just my da had this important message to do otherwise. . . . Tell her I'll call up to her house later. (*Pause.*) Will you do that?

IAN: Aye, half seven where?

BILLY: The corner of Tate's Avenue.

IAN: I'll just have to go and see the sergeant . . . it'll be all right, there'll be no problems, but I'll just have to let him know. He's a bit of a mouth you know. I'll have to change too.

BILLY: You're joking, you mean you don't want her to see you looking all lovely in your uniform?

IAN: The name's Ian, not insane.

BILLY: Are you not seeing Shirley tonight?

IAN: Aye, I'm supposed to see her at half seven. That's the time I'm off duty. Ah I'll tell her I'll see her later. I don't believe in giving women long explanations.

BILLY: I'll maybe see you if you're hanging about the corner when I get home.

IAN: Aye, all right.

10. INT. THE BOYDS' FRONT PARLOUR. EVENING

JUNE *is sitting at a table, applying lipstick. Her mother enters.* MRS BOYD *is a woman, widowed, who manifests her love and concern for* JUNE *through almost continuous nagging. She also employs a little moral blackmail by playing the ageing, helpless widow.*

MRS BOYD: So you're going out after all?

JUNE: I've arranged to meet Billy at half-past seven. I can't just stand him up.
(*Pause.*)

MRS BOYD: You realize there's been trouble all over the town today.

JUNE: I'll be careful.

MRS BOYD: Careful's not enough in this place, you have to be lucky as well. You can't be lucky all the time. I thought we could just have had a quiet night here the two of us.

JUNE: I'm sorry, Mum, but we'll have lots of nights together.

MRS BOYD: Will we . . . just over a month and you'll be away altogether. I scrimp and save and struggle to get you to university, but you can't go to the one just down the road. Not you, it has to be half-way across the world to suit you.

JUNE: Half-way across the world . . . York?

MRS BOYD: What's wrong with Queen's, I'd like to know.

JUNE: There's nothing wrong with Queen's, I just want to get away.

MRS BOYD: Now you're off out tonight and all this trouble. Anything could happen . . . you could be killed, then what would I do?

JUNE: Sure Mrs Cooper'll come in and sit with you.

MRS BOYD: And I'd have to sit and listen to the history of her aches and pains, no thank you. If you were never ill that woman would make you think you were dying. (*Pause.*) Billy this and Billy that . . . you go and see Billy. I'll watch television, or read. It'll be practice for when you're not here at all.

JUNE: (*Pouting her lips*) What do you think of this lipstick?

MRS BOYD: It's all right . . . let's hope it's still on your lips when you get back.

11. EXT. THE STREET CORNER. EVENING

IAN *is standing there. He has changed.* SHIRLEY *approaches.*

SHIRLEY: I thought you didn't come off until half seven?

IAN: Aye, I had to get off a wee bit early. I've a message to do.

SHIRLEY: What sort of message?

IAN: Just a message, for a mate.

SHIRLEY: What about me? You're supposed to see me at half seven.

IAN: I'll be a wee bit late . . . not much mind. I'll see you at half eight.

SHIRLEY: Half eight . . . that's a bloody hour.

IAN: Between half eight and a quarter to nine.

SHIRLEY: Aye, keep it up. It'll soon be between half eleven and a quarter to twelve. It's Saturday night you know. I'm not going to hang about waiting for you all night. What's this message anyway?

IAN: It's nothing, love. Very hush-hush. Look I promise I'll be here by half eight.

SHIRLEY: If you're not here by a quarter past eight . . . forget it.

IAN: Ah, love . . .

SHIRLEY: Never mind the 'Ah, love' bit. I've heard it all before. If you're not here there'll be trouble.

12. INT. THE MARTINS' LIVING ROOM. EVENING

BILLY *is ready to go out.* LORNA *hands him a sheet of paper.*

LORNA: Here, take this.

(*He opens it.*)

BILLY: What is it?

LORNA: Maureen made her a birthday card.

BILLY: Her birthday's not for over a week.

LORNA: Yes . . . I'd like her to have it . . . I'd like her to know . . . (*Cries.*)

BILLY (*comforts her.*)

(ANN *comes in from the scullery.*)

ANN: What is it . . . what's wrong?

(*Pause.*)

LORNA: Have you all of those dishes done?

ANN: Yes . . .

BILLY: I'm away . . . don't forget that wee girl.

LORNA: You be careful, Billy. I wish you'd give June a miss for tonight.

BILLY: I'll be all right. I'll see you later.

(*He goes.* LORNA *and* ANN *sit. They don't speak.*)

13. EXT. THE BANK AT THE CORNER OF TATE'S AVENUE. EVENING

JUNE *is standing. She checks her watch.* IAN *approaches, stops with her. They speak for a moment. He has obviously given her the message.*

JUNE: Well . . . thanks for coming up and letting me know.

IAN: No trouble. (*Pause.*) Look, ah, why don't I walk you back up home?

JUNE: No, it's quite all right. It's not far.

IAN: Still, the oul troubles and all. I think Billy'd expect me to see you home safe.

JUNE: It's all right really . . . there's no need to.

IAN: No, I insist. Billy and me's best mates. (*Putting an arm round her*) You'll be all right with me.

JUNE: (*Gently but firmly removing his arm*) I think it's better if we just walk together . . . in case you would trip, and pull me down with you.

(*They move off together.*)

14. INT. THE WAITING ROOM BESIDE THE SIDE-WARD. EVENING

BILLY *is sitting gazing into space.* TWO NURSES *emerge from the side-ward. They are pushing a laundry skip. One nods to* BILLY *and holds the door for him. He gathers himself, as if going in is an effort of will. He passes in. The* NURSES *exchange a sympathetic glance and leave. Zoom in on the doors.*

15. INT. THE MARTINS' LIVING ROOM. EVENING

LORNA *and* ANN *are still sitting.*

ANN: What will happen if Billy marries June and leaves? What will happen to us?

LORNA: We'll just have to manage without him.

ANN: Would you like him to marry her?

(*Long pause.*)

LORNA: No.

ANN: She wants him to go to England with her. Do you hate her?

LORNA: No, of course not.

ANN: Does he love her?

LORNA: I don't know. I don't think he knows.

ANN: Why do you not go out with boys?

(LORNA *is visibly upset, but doesn't reply. Pause.*)

16. INT. THE BOYDS' FRONT PARLOUR. EVENING

JUNE *enters, followed by her* MOTHER.

MRS BOYD: Stood you up. That's a fine way to behave. Who does he think he is, standing up a daughter of mine?

JUNE: Mother, he did not stand me up. He sent his friend to tell me.

MRS BOYD: Sent his friend!

JUNE: He went to a great deal of trouble to let me know. (*Pause.*) He's coming up here later.

MRS BOYD: Up here . . . tonight? What for?

JUNE: To see me . . . to talk.

MRS BOYD: Really, June . . . you know I don't like him up here.

JUNE: You're a snob, Mother.

MRS BOYD: I am not a snob. It's just . . . he's a boy I find it difficult to talk to. (*Pause.*) Your father . . . well, we both wanted the best for you.

JUNE: Is telly good tonight?

MRS BOYD: Stands you up and then announces that he's going to stroll in here at all hours of the night. He wouldn't have done it in your father's time.

JUNE: Mother!

MRS BOYD: I'm just saying . . .

JUNE: Mother, I wasn't old enough for boyfriends in my father's time.

MRS BOYD: He wanted the best for you. He wouldn't have approved of Master Billy Martin.

JUNE: There's nothing wrong with Billy.

MRS BOYD: Nothing wrong. . . ! He wouldn't have been allowed in over that door in your father's day.

JUNE: Please. What did you do when I was out?

MRS BOYD: Well, I'd just turned the television off and settled down with a book, when Mrs Cooper called. Her sister's dropped in, and she'd run out of milk.

JUNE: She can't have stayed long.

MRS BOYD: Long enough to tell me about all her aches and pains. If that woman spent less time sitting on her own moping, if she'd get out more, she'd have fewer aches and pains.

JUNE: She's doing what you're threatening to do when I go.

MRS BOYD: Me! God forbid, you'd think that woman was in her seventies.

JUNE: Isn't she?

MRS BOYD: She is not, she's just a year or two older than I am. Her man ran after her too much, that was her trouble. God help him, there he is, gone this ten years and she's still here.

JUNE: I'd hate to see you like her.

MRS BOYD: Me . . . no fear . . . I'll be . . .
(*Looks at* JUNE, *who is smiling.*)
It's only to have you here with me . . .

JUNE: I know . . . but sure if York doesn't work out after the first year . . .

MRS BOYD: You just remember you've got a home here. I want no daughter of mine starving herself, or sleeping in a dirty bed. (*Pause.*) What about a cup of tea while you're waiting for Romeo?

JUNE: Lovely . . .

17. INT. THE HOSPITAL. EVENING

BILLY *emerges from the side-ward. It should be obvious that the visit has been painful for him. He almost lies against the door. Punches the doorpost. He looks back into the side-ward. Turns, shakes his head. He moves slowly to a chair. He sits, and then with a long sigh he spreads himself out in the chair. He rests his neck on the back of the chair, gazing at the ceiling.*

18. INT. THE MARTINS' LIVING ROOM. EVENING

MAUREEN: Lorna, who was Stevie?

LORNA: Stevie! (*Pause.*) I don't know.

MAUREEN: Mummy kept on about somebody called Stevie.

LORNA: I thought you said she went on about Dad?

MAUREEN: She did, but about Stevie as well. Him and Daddy. Who was he?

LORNA: She just rambles. She doesn't know what she's saying.

MAUREEN: She looked at me. You know the way she just rambles on, and then seems just to notice you're there and she says something straight to you. She just looked at me and said, 'I loved Stevie, but Norman couldn't understand that.' Then she started to cry and I couldn't make her out any more. (*Pause.*) Who was he, Lorna?

LORNA: He was an insurance man who called every Friday night.

ANN: He was her boyfriend.

LORNA: For goodness' sake, Ann.

ANN: It's true, isn't it?

LORNA: It was a long time ago.

(*Quick fade.*)

19. INT. THE MARTINS' LIVING ROOM. EVENING

Flashback. The living room some years earlier. JANET *is sitting, dressed up.* STEVIE *enters, insurance books under his arm. He is tall, thinnish, a bit younger than* JANET, *but not much. As soon as he enters, he puts the books down, she rises and they embrace.*

STEVIE: Come to the man who will 'insure' your happiness.

JANET: You're late.

STEVIE: Unavoidably detained, one of those nights when nobody seems to have any change. (*In mock Scottish accent*) Where's No . . . r . . . man?

JANET: Where he always is. I thought you were going to be too late. Young Billy's at a football match with his Uncle Andy.

STEVIE: I thought they went to bed early?

JANET: They do, but this is a birthday treat.

STEVIE: Is it young Billy's birthday?

JANET: No, it's Andy's. He always has a few drinks on his birthday. I always send him a card, which reminds him he's got a sister. Then he calls over and makes some vague wee generous gesture.

STEVIE: It isn't much, what does it cost for a youngster, ten, or fifteen pence?

JANET: Good grief, he's not that generous. It's taking him that's the gesture. He lifts him over. I even had to give him the money for a programme.

STEVIE: (*Grabbing her again*) Well let's not waste our time. (*Kisses her again.*) We'll have to stop meeting like this darling. We'll have to change our 'policy'. Did you do what I told you?

JANET: I was at the doctor today.

STEVIE: Yes . . . well?

JANET: Oh, he wants me to go for tests. Probably nothing he says, but best to be on the safe side.

STEVIE: There can't be anything wrong with you darling, because you grow more beautiful all the time. (*Pulls her closer.*) I love you.

(*Kisses her. Giggling is heard on the stairs. They break, embarrassed. Feet are heard scampering up the stairs.* JANET *goes to the foot of the stairs.*)

JANET: Lorna! Ann! If you two aren't asleep in two minutes I'll go up with the belt. (*Pause.*) Bitches.

STEVIE: Will they tell?

JANET: No, no. I'll tell them it was only a joke or something. They're only youngsters.

STEVIE: (*Very worried*) But it might come out . . . they mightn't realize . . . good grief.

JANET: Oh come on . . . stop worrying.

STEVIE: I only sell insurance, love, I don't buy any.

JANET: Listen, they wouldn't say anything that might cause trouble. Relax. (*Laughs.*) I'll 'insure' we aren't discovered. (*He smiles at her. They embrace again and are kissing when the door crashes open and* NORMAN *is there.* JANET *screams as* NORMAN *lunges at* STEVIE.)

20. INT. THE MARTINS' LIVING ROOM. EVENING

Back in the present.

MAUREEN: What did Daddy do?

ANN: He put Stevie bloody Wonder in hospital for six weeks, and he deserved it. It's all her fault. She used to tart herself up and go out to dances. That's what all the big rows were about.

MAUREEN: What was Stevie like? Was he nice?

LORNA: I don't remember.

(*Pause.*)

ANN: He wasn't when my da was finished with him. It was awful. Dad kept pushing his face against the wall. Then he punched my ma one, right on the mouth.

LORNA: He walked out then and didn't come back for two weeks.

ANN: That's why he doesn't visit her. I was with him and she said she loved Stevie, she said it to him. I thought he was going to cry . . . or kill her.

LORNA: It was a long time ago. People fall in love, it doesn't . . . (*Pause.*) It started when Dad was in England. With his brother, Uncle Herbie, the builder. Dad worked for him.

ANN: She started him drinking heavy. She was always saying stupid things to men, and laughing when they said stupid things to her. Every time you went out with her she'd stop to talk to some man. The whole street talked about her, laughed at us. Laughed at my da.

LORNA: Why should we care about the whole street?

ANN: Well I do. They tell you you look just like your ma, and then snigger about it. I'm glad my da gets drunk and knocks the shit out of them, and our Billy. It's all her fault, she was an oul whore.

LORNA: That's enough, Ann. Just leave it. It's over and done with. (*Pause.*) It's not as if she'll ever do it again.

ANN: Why did he come back at all after those two weeks?

LORNA: For us, he said.

MAUREEN: Then why does he hit us?

LORNA: It's the drink. (*Pause.*) Men think all about the past when they're drunk.

ANN: I hate that oul bitch. You should have seen his face that day she said it. He looked at me . . . and I knew he hated me for hearing it. (*Pause.*) Why couldn't we have a nice ma and da like Sally Johnston has?

MAUREEN: Ugh . . . they're stupid. They kiss at the door and walk about holding hands.

LORNA: That's what you do when you're in love.

MAUREEN: Ugh . . . but they're married and old.

ANN: They hardly even shout at her, and her da's never hit her.

MAUREEN: He wears an apron on Sundays and hoovers.

LORNA: Could you picture our dad in an apron?

(*They laugh.*)

ANN: With a wee feather duster . . .

MAUREEN: Out brushing the front . . .

LORNA: Could you picture them all round here if he did that?

ANN: If anybody said anything . . .

MAUREEN: Or laughed . . .

ANN: He'd ram the brush up their arses . . .

(*They laugh.*)

21. EXT. PUBLIC HOUSE. EVENING

NORMAN *comes out—a little unsteady on his feet. Goes off.*

22. INT. HOSPITAL WAITING ROOM. EVENING

BILLY *gathers himself. He goes and looks through the windows again. Holds a moment. Turns away. Leaves.*

23. EXT. DIFFERENT PUBLIC HOUSE. EVENING

NORMAN *comes along—enters the public house.*

24. INT. THE BOYDS' FRONT PARLOUR. EVENING

JUNE *enters with* BILLY. *They kiss.*

BILLY: Where is she?

JUNE: At the loo. She'll have heard the door and not be able to get down quickly enough. (*Pause.*) How are you?

BILLY: I'm great, what about yourself?

JUNE: Great too. When you didn't turn up . . . when I saw him . . . How is your mother?

BILLY: Oh she's marvellous. Didn't you hear she played hockey today? It's true, cancer patients versus the rest. They were doing all right, until their sticks were removed. They thought they were malignant.

JUNE: I only asked. (*Pause.*) There's no need to be like that about it.

BILLY: I'm sick of it. Every time I walk down the street they ask the same questions, and say the same stupid bloody things. Nobody cared much before. I've told you we're the joke family, remember? The drunken da, and the playgirl ma.

JUNE: Why do you resent sympathy? (*Pause.*) That horrid friend of yours tried to pick me up.

BILLY: Ian? He couldn't pick up flu in an epidemic.

(*Pause.* MRS BOYD *enters.*)

MRS BOYD: Oh, you got here. I thought I heard the door.

BILLY: How are you, Mrs Boyd?

MRS BOYD: I'm the same as usual . . . just the same. (*Pause.*) I don't suppose you'll be staying long . . . in count of the trouble?

BILLY: It's pretty quiet now, I think.

MRS BOYD: That's until the pubs get out. If they'd put a stop to the drinking. June's father always said it rotted men's minds. The root of all evil he called it.

BILLY: I thought that was what money was supposed to be?

MRS BOYD: It's a mystery to me how the half of them can afford it. June's father never let a drop pass his lips.

BILLY: I don't drink either, Mrs Boyd.

MRS BOYD: Oh . . . have you stopped?

BILLY: I've never started.

MRS BOYD: Oh, well, you're a very wise young man. June's father always used to say that when the drunk man staggered in through the door, happiness left by the window. But of course you'd know all about that.

JUNE: Dad was a fund of knowledge.

MRS BOYD: He was a very clever, sober man. (*Long pause.*) Do you go to church, Billy?

BILLY: Ah . . . no . . . no I don't.

MRS BOYD: You should. It's a great comfort in times of trouble.

BILLY: Yes, it must be.

MRS BOYD: How is your mother?

BILLY: She's very . . . (*Pause.*) She's very weak.

MRS BOYD: It's a terrible thing. Poor woman. (*Pause.*) I had a cousin had the same thing.

BILLY: Yes . . . you told me about him before.

MRS BOYD: Him? Oh no, Myrtle . . . our Myrtle had the same thing as your poor mother. Just thirty-six and with a young family.

JUNE: Mother . . . Billy will have to go soon, and we'd like to talk.

MRS BOYD: Yes . . . well I suppose . . . (*Pause.*) She was just over four stone when the Lord decided to call her. (*Pause.*) You should pray, Billy.

BILLY: I am, Mrs Boyd . . . hard.

MRS BOYD: I believe in prayer, son . . . but she laughs at me. You're not a Christian, Billy?

JUNE: Mother . . . please. Billy doesn't have time for all this now.

MRS BOYD: Many a time prayer has worked when the doctors have given up.

BILLY: I must use your toilet.

JUNE: Would you like some tea?

BILLY: What?

JUNE: Pardon?

BILLY: (*Going*) The toilet . . .

(*Pause.*)

JUNE: Mother, would you please go to bed without saying another word to Billy . . . please?

MRS BOYD: I was only trying to . . .

JUNE: I know, I know. He's just left his mother's bedside . . . he's very upset and it's the very last thing he wants to talk about.

MRS BOYD: Oh dear, was I tactless?

JUNE: He understands . . . but it's upsetting . . . it's just . . .

MRS BOYD: He says he prays.

JUNE: He's probably doing it right now.

MRS BOYD: What, in the bathroom? Surely he wouldn't pray from there? It's hardly decent.

JUNE: Come on, Mother. (*Rises.*) I'm going to make Billy a cup of tea while you boil your milk.

(*They go. Pause.* BILLY *returns. He crosses to the mantelpiece and stares at the Boyds' wedding photograph. He replaces it as* JUNE *enters.*)

BILLY: Has she gone?

JUNE: Yes . . . I've a cup of tea on for you. I've just to take up her cup of chocolate and then I'll be in with the tea . . .

(*They kiss.*)

25. INT. THE HOSPITAL. EVENING

NORMAN *staggers in and goes up to gaze into the side-ward. He wipes his eyes. After a moment a* NURSE *enters and speaks to him. She gently takes his arm and leads him out. Zoom in on side-ward.* JANET *watches him go, tears in her eyes.*

26. INT. THE MARTINS' LIVING ROOM. EVENING

MAUREEN *is curled up in a chair. She is dressed for bed, reading a book.* LORNA *is polishing a pair of shoes. Another pair, already clean, sits beside her. Two pairs, uncleaned, are on her other side.* ANN *emerges from the scullery.*

ANN: Will I use butter or marge on the toast?

LORNA: Marge, and don't put too much tea in the pot. Hurry up, I don't want you still at your supper when Dad comes in.

27. EXT. STREET CORNER. NIGHT

IAN *and* SHIRLEY *emerge from the entry and walk to the corner. They are having a row.*

SHIRLEY: You needn't think you can turn up too late to take me anywhere and just get that.

IAN: I've told you I got back as quick as I could.

SHIRLEY: Going to see his bloody girlfriend for him. If I'd known that's where you were going I wouldn't have waited for you.

IAN: I just walked up with her. It was just the nice thing to do.

SHIRLEY: When do you ever do the nice thing for me?

IAN: Ah come on . . . didn't I bring you a present from Bangor last week?

SHIRLEY: (*Groping in her bag and bringing out a small compact*) Present you call it . . . you got it cheap because the oul mirror was cracked. You probably looked in it.
(*She flings it against the wall.*)

IAN: Ah you lousy wee bitch . . . that cost me money.
(*He gets down on his hands and knees to retrieve the pieces.*)

SHIRLEY: You can count it paid for with the money you saved not taking me out the night.
(*She storms off up the street.*)

IAN: You've smashed the wee mirror . . .
(*He scrambles to his feet and starts after her.*)
Look at that . . . seven years bad luck . . .
(*A long shot of him catching up with her and her turning and kicking his leg.*)

28. INT. THE BOYDS' FRONT PARLOUR. NIGHT

BILLY *and* JUNE *are necking on the settee. He puts a hand under her blouse. Puts it round to open her bra.*

JUNE: Stop that.

BILLY: I've never been much good with bras.

JUNE: It's hardly worth the effort. I haven't got much there.
(*The heavy petting continues. He puts his hand up her skirt.*)

BILLY: Come on, June.

JUNE: No, Billy . . . we shouldn't.

BILLY: Please love. Please. Come on . . .

JUNE: Oh Billy . . . I love you asking me. I love you . . .

BILLY: Come on, June . . .

(*He pulls her on to the floor.*)

JUNE: Oh Billy . . . Billy . . . oh . . . oh . . .

BILLY: It's all right, love . . . that's it . . . that's it. It's all right, June . . .

29. INT. THE MARTINS' LIVING ROOM. NIGHT

LORNA, ANN *and* MAUREEN *are at their supper.* IAN *is with them, drinking tea.*

IAN: (*Lifting up his trousers*) Look where the bitch kicked me. (*Showing his leg.*)

ANN: Don't look so glum. This time tomorrow you'll kiss and make up.

IAN: Not this time. That's it . . . over.

LORNA: Come on, Ian, sure you two are always at it.

IAN: Naw, this is serious. She took that wee compact thing I bought her and smashed it against the wall. I mean, imagine doing a thing like that.

ANN: That's seven years' bad luck, breaking a mirror.

IAN: I told her that. She give me this boot on the leg and said she'd had the seven years' bad luck going with me. (*Pause.*)

LORNA: How did you get on with June?

IAN: Oh great, great. She was mad about me of course. But Billy's a mate, I didn't want to take her off him.

LORNA: You're so generous, Ian.

IAN: Was he back down after the hospital?

LORNA: No, he was just going on up to see June.

IAN: I'm sorry about your oul woman, a mean I always liked her . . . I know her and my ma used to be always at it . . . but . . .

(*He is becoming rather embarrassed and self-conscious. Pause. There is a loud roar from the street.*)

NORMAN'S VOICE: To hell with the hard men of Belfast.

(IAN *starts in alarm, gulps down his tea and leaps to his feet, as*

NORMAN *stumbles through the door.*)

NORMAN: Where is he?

IAN: You're all right now, Norman. You're home now. Who're you looking for?

(*He hits* IAN *on the chest and sends him crashing against the wall.*)

NORMAN: Don't you 'Norman' me. Respect . . . that's what I want, respect. What are you doing in my house?

IAN: I'm ah . . . I'm waiting for Billy . . .

NORMAN: Where is he?

IAN: He's not here, not in yet.

NORMAN: Not here . . . not in yet. He's never here. Never bloody anywhere. Up seeing her, and out with girls, isn't he, eh? Doesn't matter about me. No time for me.

(*Turns on a petrified* IAN *and grabs him.*)

D'you think I'm a fool, son, eh? Oul drunk Norman, eh? Don't you bloody 'Norman' me, or I'll put you through that bloody wall . . . you and your da.

(IAN *is whimpering.*)

It's 'Mr Martin' you call me, son . . . 'Mr Martin,' d'you hear that?

(IAN *nods.*)

LORNA: Come on, Dad. Ian'll have to go home now. His mother'll be looking for him.

NORMAN: His mother! Mother nothing . . . his bloody oul ma. Y'know your ma can't talk about nobody. She serviced half the American fleet in her day. Maybe that's how you got your yella streak.

(*He holds his fist up to* IAN*'s face.*)

You tell her if she ever talks about my wife again I'll smash her brains all over the nearest wall. You tell her my wife's a lady compared to her. You tell her my wife's near dead and she's still a better-looking woman than her.

(*Pushing* IAN *towards the door. Shouting after him as he almost falls out through it*) You tell the oul bitch that. Near dead and she's still a better-looking woman.

(*He slams the door closed. Pause.*)

LORNA: Right, come on you two, bed, quickly.

(*They rapidly finish their supper and leave.*)

NORMAN: That's right, the big bad wolf's here. You chase the kiddies off to bed. You're just like your ma.

LORNA: It's late, Dad.

(*He mimics her and swipes the abandoned dishes on to the floor.*)

NORMAN: 'It's late, Dad.' Damn the late, I'm their father. Oh, I know you might wish I wasn't, but I bloody well am. They're mine . . . my kids.

(*He staggers to the bottom of the stairs and calls out loudly.*)

Ann . . . Maureen . . . come down here.

LORNA: Dad, please.

NORMAN: Shut up. I want my children to kiss me night-night. Other mens' children kiss them. I know what you and him are trying to do. Don't think I don't know.

(*The children enter sheepishly.*)

Daddy wants a goodnight kiss.

(*The children look nervously at* LORNA. *She nods.*)

Never mind her. Never mind your big bloody sister, kiss me.

(MAUREEN *starts to cry.*)

What the hell are you crying for?

LORNA: Dad, please let them go to bed.

NORMAN: You . . . it's you. You've turned them against their own father. This is my house. I've a right to be kissed by my own kids in my own house.

(MAUREEN *cries more loudly and he shouts more loudly than ever.*)

Stop bloody crying.

LORNA: Leave them alone and let them go to bed.

NORMAN: Don't you tell me what to do. I'm sick of you telling me what to do.

(*As he goes for* LORNA, ANN *steps in between them. Before* NORMAN *realizes what is happening* ANN *kisses him on the mouth.*)

ANN: Goodnight, Daddy.

(*He stands stunned.* ANN *and* MAUREEN *go to bed. After a moment he lifts his hand and touches where she kissed.*)

LORNA: Come and sit down, Dad.

(*Pause. She takes him by the arm and he lets himself be guided into an armchair. She sits on the arm of it and strokes his head.*)

NORMAN: You're a good girl Lorna. Things happen between people . . . they just happen. (*Pause.*) Your mother and me . . . it's drink . . . drink and . . . and . . .
(*He takes her hand. He can't speak for a moment.*)
It's too late, Lorna. She's dying . . . I can't . . . can't . . . I can't talk to her. She doesn't know me. She doesn't understand what I'm saying. It is too late, love, it is.

LORNA: Talk to Billy . . . talk to him . . . it's not too late for that.

30. INT. THE BOYDS' FRONT PARLOUR. NIGHT

BILLY *and* JUNE *are sitting drinking tea. Silence.*

JUNE: You're sorry you did it, aren't you?

BILLY: It's all right.
(*Long pause.*)

JUNE: That's it, isn't it?

BILLY: June, I'm sorry.

JUNE: Thanks for bugger all. What does that make me? (*Pause.*) I pity your mother if she expects sympathy from you.

BILLY: (*Angrily*) You leave my ma out of this.

JUNE: Yes, just let you do what you like and say nothing. Why don't you hit me, Billy? Go on . . . hit me . . . that's the Martin answer to everything.

BILLY: Don't be stupid.

JUNE: I am stupid, haven't I proved that?

BILLY: I've said I'm sorry, what else can I say?

JUNE: Don't say anything, Billy. Just show me you're human.

BILLY: I don't know if I'm human any more. (*Long pause.*) I can't go away with you June . . . not now . . . not yet.

JUNE: So that was the pay-off, your big finale?

BILLY: You could go to Queen's. Give me time to sort things out.

JUNE: I could . . .

BILLY: Will you?
(*Long pause.*)

JUNE: You'd better go, Billy.
(*He rises and goes.*)
Billy for goodness' sake be careful going home.

31. INT. THE MARTINS' LIVING ROOM. NIGHT

NORMAN *is stretched out in the armchair, smoking, singing/moaning* 'Danny boy'. LORNA *is sitting sewing. She checks the time.*

32. EXT. STREET CORNER. NIGHT

IAN *is standing.* JOHN FLETCHER *staggers up.*

IAN: Right, John, what about you?

(JOHN *just nods and stands sullen.* IAN *looks uncomfortable.*)

JOHN: Where's your great mate Martin?

IAN: Billy, I don't know. I was just waiting to see if he'd come up the road.

JOHN: I'd a row with his oul fella.

IAN: He was in bad form the night.

JOHN: The oul bollocks is always in bad form. He hit me a dig on the gub.

IAN: He hit me too.

JOHN: (*With contempt for* IAN) Hit you, what for?

IAN: He was drunk.

JOHN: I just ran on to a sucker punch, otherwise I'd have given him a good go.

IAN: He's tough.

JOHN: So am I . . . you saying I'm not?

IAN: No, no, you are, John. You're one of the hardest men around here. I know that.

JOHN: I did your da one night. (*Pause.*) I said I did you da.

IAN: I know, I remember.

JOHN: You want to get me for it, eh? You want to have a go?

IAN: No, John, you give him a fair go.

(JOHN *grabs him roughly and head-butts him.* IAN*'s nose bleeds.*)

JOHN: Your oul fella was easy, and so are you.

IAN: I didn't say anything, John.

JOHN: You reckon I could take Billy?

IAN: I don't know, Billy can go some.

(JOHN *drives him against the wall.*)

JOHN: Could he take me?

IAN: Aaagh . . . I don't know, John. (*Pause.*) Please, John, don't hit me.

JOHN: I'm going to kick your shite in.
(*Starts to drag him round the corner.*)
Come on round the entry.

IAN: Ah, please, John, I never said anything, please.

JOHN: You're his mate.
(BILLY *arrives on the scene.*)

BILLY: What's going on?

JOHN: Oh, it's the Boy Wonder himself. Your great mate fancies his chances.

IAN: I don't . . . aaagh . . . I never said a word, Billy. I was just standing waiting for you, I never said a thing.

BILLY: Leave him alone.
(JOHN *slowly lets go of* IAN.)

JOHN: Is that an order?

BILLY: It's good advice.
(*Pause. They glare at each other.* JOHN *is not so sure any more.*)

JOHN: I'd a row with your da.

BILLY: He must have took pity on you if you're still able to stand.

JOHN: He hit me a lucky blow, before I was ready.

BILLY: My da could beat you with his cap.
(BILLY *is anxious to avoid a fight, but he can't show any sign of weakness. This would seem like fear, and restore* FLETCHER*'s confidence.*)

JOHN: You Martins all think you're hard men, don't you?

BILLY: That's right, and we don't have to dress up to prove it.

JOHN: Someday you'll push your luck too far.

BILLY: Any time you want . . . like right now.
(*Pause.*)

JOHN: (*Laughing*) Look, Billy oul son, I've had a bit too much.
(*He pulls a large bottle of wine from his pocket.* BILLY *instinctively steps back a bit.*)
Trust me, Billy. Listen . . . a wee drink, eh?

BILLY: I don't.

JOHN: Come on, a wee slug won't hurt you. It was your oul fella I was mad at, but he got me a good one. Fair and square, he laid me out.

(*Offers the bottle.*)

BILLY: I've told you I don't.

JOHN: It's an insult to refuse a drink.

(*He puts his other hand in his pocket.* BILLY *notices this.*)

BILLY: All right . . . just one swig.

(BILLY *takes the bottle and crashes it down on* JOHN*'s skull.* JOHN *slumps to the ground.* BILLY *checks the pocket his hand went into and removes a flick-knife.*)

IAN: I think the rotten bastard's broke my nose.

BILLY: You don't gain anything trying to reason with the likes of him. You're better just lashing out and taking your chances. (*Pause.*) I'm away up.

IAN: Are you going to leave him there?

BILLY: Why not, you don't think I'm going to take him home with me do you?

IAN: Should we not drag him into the entry out of the way?

BILLY: You do it if you like . . . he's your sergeant.

(BILLY *goes.* IAN *starts to drag* JOHN. *He dumps him in the entry and comes back out.*)

IAN: (*Feeling his nose*) Bastard . . .

(*He turns and goes back into the entry. The thuds can be heard as he kicks* JOHN.)

33. INT. THE MARTINS' LIVING ROOM. NIGHT

NORMAN *sits up as* BILLY *enters.*

LORNA: Billy, where on earth have you been, it's after half two.

BILLY: I got held up.

LORNA: There's no trouble is there?

BILLY: No, not a thing. All quiet in West Belfast.

(*Pause.*)

LORNA: How's Mum?

(*He just shakes his head.*)

NORMAN: I couldn't get away.

BILLY: I'll have to write to your agent and see if we can book you for the funeral.

LORNA: (*Quickly*) Would you like something to eat, Billy?

BILLY: You just go on to bed. I'll make myself a cup of tea.

LORNA: No, I'll do it.

NORMAN: (*Rising*) I'm going to bed.

LORNA: Would you like some tea, Dad?

NORMAN: No, I don't want any of your tea. (*To* BILLY) I was going to go up and see her tonight. I did . . . I had to see a man.

BILLY: Hurry up with that tea, Lorna.

NORMAN: Are you listening to me?

BILLY: (*To* LORNA) Give me a round of bread and jam.

NORMAN: (*Grabbing* BILLY) I'm talking to you.

BILLY: (*Pulling roughly away from him*) Why don't you go up to the hospital and talk to your wife?

NORMAN: Look, I'm trying to tell you. I'm trying to explain.

BILLY: Don't tell me, I don't want your explanations. Go up and tell her.

LORNA: Billy!

NORMAN: Tell him to listen to me.

BILLY: Why don't you tell me when you're sober . . . if I live that long.

NORMAN: I don't want any of your bloody lip, boy.

BILLY: You might frighten those kids upstairs, but you don't frighten me.

NORMAN: I'm not trying to frighten anybody. (*To* LORNA) For Christ's sake tell him to listen to me. I'm trying to talk to him.

BILLY: You're about sixteen years too late.

LORNA: Billy, let him speak.

BILLY: I don't want to hear him. Go to bed, old man. Go to bed and rest up for your wife's funeral.

NORMAN: I'll bloody kill you.

LORNA: Billy, the kids have had enough for one night. (*Pause.*) Dad, look, leave it for tonight. Go up to bed and I'll bring you up some tea.

NORMAN: Shove your tea up your arse. You're always on his side. He's in the wrong, but you won't admit it. No, it's always my fault. Tell him, why don't you tell him he's in the wrong?

BILLY: Me in the wrong! What are you mouthing about you drunken idiot? You haven't been up to see my ma for over a week.

NORMAN: Your ma. You, and her, and your ma. I wish the whole bloody lot of you had cancer. I wish you were all bloody dying. I go out to work every day. Your ma never knew what it was like to have a broken pay.

BILLY: No, but she knew what it was like to have a broken jaw, and a broken nose.

NORMAN: I'm warning you, I'm bloody warning you.

BILLY: Why didn't you let her run off with her insurance man?

LORNA: For goodness' sake, Billy.

BILLY: He was a better bloody man than you. At least he appreciated her. But you couldn't take that. She loved him. She despised you, but she loved him.

(NORMAN *grabs him by the throat and knees him repeatedly, bellowing as he does so.*)

34. EXT. THE MARTINS' BACKYARD. EVENING

Flashback. NORMAN *has a fistful of* STEVIE*'s hair at the back. He keeps smashing* STEVIE*'s face into the wall.* JANET *attacks him, screaming. He drops* STEVIE *to the ground, turns and smashes his fist into* JANET*'s face. She falls back into the scullery, flat out. He turns and starts to kick at* STEVIE.

35. INT. THE MARTINS' LIVING ROOM. NIGHT

STEVIE *turns into* BILLY.

NORMAN: I'll kill you, you wee bastard. I'll kill you.

(LORNA *frantically tries to pull him off. When he stops,* BILLY *is rolling on the floor moaning.* LORNA *slaps* NORMAN*'s face. He grabs her hair and jerks her head back.*)

Don't you ever lift your hand to me again, or I'll break your bloody neck.

(*He pushes her aside, pulls* BILLY *to his feet, drags him to the door. He throws him out into the street.* ANN *and* MAUREEN *start crying.*)

If you ever come back into this house, I'll kill you.

36. EXT. THE MARTINS' HOUSE. NIGHT

NORMAN *slams the door.* BILLY *falling on to the pavement and the front door slamming shut.*

NORMAN *(VO)* Shut up, up there. Do you hear me? Shut bloody up.

(BILLY *lies there.*)

37. INT. THE MARTINS' SCULLERY. EVENING

Flashback. JANET *lying flat out on the scullery floor, her mouth and nose bleeding.*

38. INT. HOSPITAL. NIGHT

JANET *lying in the hospital bed, ashen, emaciated face and body. Staring blankly.*

39. INT. THE MARTINS' LIVING ROOM. NIGHT

NORMAN, *cigarette in hand, slumped in his chair, gazing at the ceiling.*

40. INT. THE MARTINS' SCULLERY. NIGHT

LORNA, *in the scullery, crying silently, tears coursing down her cheeks. She is clearing up a few dishes.*

41. EXT. STREET CORNER. NIGHT

BILLY *at the deserted corner. He stands for a moment, turns and limps off.*

42. INT. THE MARTINS' LIVING ROOM. DAY

NORMAN *is just finishing his breakfast, laid out on a small, folding, card table.* LORNA *is taking a cup of tea.*

NORMAN: What day's this? Tuesday, isn't it?

LORNA: Yes.

NORMAN: Any word of that Billy fella?

LORNA: He called in yesterday.

NORMAN: Sneaked in when I was out?

LORNA: He shouldn't have to sneak in, it's his home.

NORMAN: When he's bringing in a wage to pay the rent it'll be his home.

LORNA: He gives all he can.

NORMAN: The dole won't keep a home.

LORNA: He does his bit, Dad, you know that.
(*Pause.*)

NORMAN: I writ to my brother Herbie a while ago. That letter yesterday . . . it was from him.

LORNA: I saw the Birmingham postmark.

NORMAN: He's a job for me . . . as soon as I want to go.

LORNA: And are you going to?

NORMAN: Why not? Damn all for me here. (*Pause.*) I'll be away as soon as we see your ma off. (*Pause.*) I'll not be back.

LORNA: We shouldn't give up hope. Mother might recover . . . God's good.

NORMAN: God's a bollocks!

LORNA: Dad! God forgive you!

NORMAN: (*Mimicking*) 'God's good . . . God forgive you . . . God bless you . . . God is love.' Whoever he loves, it isn't this family. He's never done nothing for us.

LORNA: You have to have faith.

NORMAN: Faith, my arse. All your praying and church-going hasn't done her much good. (*Pause.*) When I was young I was dragged out to church every Sunday morning; pushed out to Sunday School every Sunday afternoon; dragged back to church every Sunday night. My mother was the closest thing to a saint you'll ever see. My da was a drunken waster. Before she got out to church on a Sunday morning she'd have to wash the spew from him and put him to bed. He died in his sleep one Tuesday night, with a smile on his face. (*Pause.*) Do you know what happened to her?

LORNA: You've told me.

NORMAN: Well I'll tell you again . . . she lay for months in agony. I heard her praying . . . for relief. I heard her praying to die. For the last week of her life she screamed at God to help her. There was no smile on her face when she died. Her face was twisted up in pain. (*Pause.*) Don't you tell me God is good, girl.

LORNA: Maybe the reason's not for us to know.

NORMAN: Aye, he's a great one for keeping secrets, is God. Do you know what my aunt Chrissie told me? She said God was trying to spare me. He didn't want me to mourn my mother, so he made it that awful I'd be glad to see her going. Did you ever hear such a load of oul bollocks in your life?

LORNA: I wish you wouldn't talk like that. You never know what might happen to you when you step out of that door.

NORMAN: I know I'll not trip over a brand new Datsun, like your Reverent Woods.

LORNA: The Reverent Woods is a very good man. He's been a great comfort to Mother.

NORMAN: After she's had her injection Santa Claus would be a great comfort to her. I'll tell you what . . . you put your Reverent Woods on one side of the bed, and the doctor with her injection on the other, and see which one she turns to first.

(*Pause.*)

LORNA: Would you like some more tea?

NORMAN: (*Draining his cup*) Aye . . . a half cup.

(*She takes his cup and goes into the scullery to refill it. He starts tying his boots. She returns.*)

LORNA: Dad?

NORMAN: I said half a cup, that's three-quarters. (*Sips.*) What?

LORNA: Can Billy come back?

NORMAN: I've told you I'm going. After that you and him's in charge.

(*Pause.*)

LORNA: He'll have to come up soon for clothes, but I'd like him back.

NORMAN: Where's he staying anyway?

LORNA: He's with Uncle Andy.

NORMAN: Huh, I wouldn't wish that oul bollocks even on him. Does he still fart and blame the cat? (*Pause.*) Tell him he can come back . . . that I'll be going away soon.

LORNA: Thanks, Dad.

(*She goes into the scullery. He rises, drains his cup, combs his hair, and puts on his jacket and overcoat. She returns with his lunchbox.*)

NORMAN: What's in them?

LORNA: Chicken paste.

NORMAN: Is there a bun for my tea break?

LORNA: There's two custards.

NORMAN: It's time you got yourself a boyfriend you know . . . you can't waste your own life on the others. (*Pause.*) Don't tell them two young ones I'm goin', not until nearer the time.

(*He stands with the door open, ready to go. She kisses him on the cheek.*)

LORNA: Take care of yourself, Dad.

NORMAN: I'm only going to the bloody shipyard, not the Western Front.

(*He goes. She comes into the centre of the room. Regards herself in the mirror. She goes to the sideboard, removes a wedding photograph of her mother and father. She places it on the mantelshelf and regards it for a moment. She removes it, kisses it and replaces it in the drawer. She begins to clear up the breakfast things.*)

43. EXT. ENTRANCE TO BOTANIC GARDENS. DAY

BILLY *and* LORNA *emerge from the front gates of the botanic gardens. They cross the road and stroll up college gardens. Fade up on dialogue.*

LORNA: Ian's gone. Nobody knows where he is, just disappeared. John Fletcher has a fractured skull. The police are at his bedside.

BILLY: Do they know what happened to him?

LORNA: They know he was hit over the head, probably with a bottle, but he was kicked as well. Apparently he could be barely recognized. His face was kicked to a pulp.

BILLY: Will he live?

LORNA: Nobody knows. It happened on Saturday. This is Tuesday and he's still unconscious. It could have been you, walking over to Uncle Andy's at that time of night.

BILLY: I was all right, I'm not involved in anything.

LORNA: What does that matter? What did he say to you?

BILLY: Oh the usual . . . about his poor sister and the bad man she married.

LORNA: I could laugh at him and his 'poor sister' bit, he never had much time for her . . .

44. EXT. LISBURN ROAD/CITY HOSPITAL. DAY

BILLY *and* LORNA *walk across the Lisburn Road, and into the grounds of the city hospital. Fade up on dialogue.*

BILLY: And my da said I could come back?

LORNA: Yes. (*Pause.*) It was terrible after he'd gone to bed on Saturday. I heard him arguing with himself . . . and then he started crying.

BILLY: He must have got all the draws and forgot to post the coupon.

LORNA: He's like a bear with a thorn in its paw, and he doesn't know how to get it out.

BILLY: We should be drilling through from the top of his head.

LORNA: He really did want to talk to you the other night. I wish you'd listened.

BILLY: We can't talk, Lorna. Maybe we should phone each other or something.

LORNA: You can maybe add a few lines to the bottom of my letters when he goes away?

BILLY: Aye . . . maybe. (*Pause.*) When he hands over to me.

45. INT. SIDE-WARD. DAY

BILLY *and* LORNA *approach the side-ward.*

LORNA: Billy . . .

(*They stop.*)

Do you believe in God?

(BILLY, *gazing through the side-ward window. He looks back at* LORNA.)

BILLY: No.

LORNA: What do you think of people who do?

BILLY: They're lucky.

(*They pass into the side-ward.*)

46. INT. THE MARTINS' LIVING ROOM. DAY

BILLY *and* LORNA *are taking a cup of tea.* ANN *and* MAUREEN *enter.*

BILLY: Hello, girls.

ANN: Billy, have you moved back in?

BILLY: Yep.

ANN: Great, how was life with Uncle Andy?

BILLY: It's a great way to slim. By the time he's finished spitting his lungs up into the fire, and taking his teeth out and setting them beside his plate, the appetite just leaves you.

LORNA: Oh, Billy . . .

MAUREEN: I'm away out again, Lorna.

LORNA: You watch where you're going, and be in for your tea. (MAUREEN *goes.*)

BILLY: How's school, Ann?

ANN: Ugh. The Concorde says I've to get my da to sign all my homeworks.

BILLY: Who's the Concorde?

ANN: Mr Williamson. You should see his hooter. When he's turned sideways he looks just like the Concorde. I told him my da wouldn't do it, but he says it has to be him or my ma, nobody else.

LORNA: I'll sign Dad's name, sure he'll never know the difference.

ANN: With a snout like his he'd smell a rat at twenty thousand feet.

BILLY: You should have asked him round to meet my da. Being a teacher he probably thinks most das are human.

ANN: I'd love to. My da'd probably get him by the big snout and swing him round his head.

LORNA: Why does he want your homework signed all of a sudden?

ANN: It's just about ten of us. He said our attitude was . . . what was it now? . . . submersive, or something daft like that.

LORNA: Do you not think we've enough to worry about without any trouble from the school?

ANN: It's not my fault.

LORNA: You keep out of trouble. If he sends a note home to Dad, you're dead. Is he new?

ANN: Aye . . . he's a drip and he thinks he's lovely. Keeps chatting up Miss Baker. It's a laugh. Sandra Mercer said to

Miss Baker the other day, 'Excuse me, Miss Baker, have you ever had a ride by Concorde?' We were killing ourselves, but she didn't catch on. 'As a matter of fact, Mercer, I was thinking of trying it next summer.'

LORNA: I'm warning you, Ann, don't get into any trouble up there. (*Pause.*) Are you going up again, Billy?

BILLY: Aye, I'd better.

ANN: Are you not seeing June?

BILLY: No . . . not tonight.

ANN: Why do you never bring her down now, Billy?

BILLY: She's going away soon.

(*Long pause.*)

ANN: Are you going with her?

LORNA: Never mind all the questions Ann, you'd . . .

BILLY: No . . . I'm staying here.

(*He looks at* LORNA. *They smile.*)

47. EXT. STREET. DAY

BILLY *coming down the street. He meets* ANN *on her way home from school. They speak. She appears to break down and go racing up the street. He continues down the street.*

48. INT. THE MARTINS' LIVING ROOM. DAY

LORNA *is tidying.* ANN *tumbles in upset. She drops her schoolbag. They gaze at each other for a moment. Pause.*

ANN: Is she dead?

LORNA: Not quite . . . Billy's away up.

ANN: I saw him . . . he wouldn't say . . . where's my da?

LORNA: He's not home yet. They've sent for him.

ANN: Is he still going away?

LORNA: Yes.

ANN: I don't want him to go. Who'll look after him over there?

LORNA: Sush, love . . . let's get this bit over first.

ANN: Are we going up?

LORNA: Billy says no. (*Pause.*) I'd rather not anyway.

(*Pause.* ANN *collapses into* LORNA*'s arms.*)

49. INT. SIDE-WARD. EVENING

BILLY *outside the side-ward. A* NURSE *opens the door of the side-ward and beckons him in.*

50. INT. THE MARTINS' LIVING ROOM. EVENING

JUNE *is there.*

JUNE: Do you think it would be all right?

LORNA: It'll be all right . . . he'll be glad of someone. (*Pause.*) I can't . . .
(*Pause.*)

JUNE: Thank you . . .
(*She goes.*)

51. INT. SIDE-WARD. EVENING

NORMAN *gazes through the side-ward window. After a moment he enters.* BILLY *looks up at him.* NORMAN *looks at the bed.*

52. INT. THE MARTINS' LIVING ROOM. EVENING

Flashback. NORMAN *sees* JANET *laughing.*

53. INT. THE SCULLERY. EVENING

Flashback. JANET *lying on the scullery floor bleeding.*

54. INT. SIDE-WARD. EVENING

JANET *as she is—dead.*

BILLY: You've mistimed it again. You're too late to talk to her, and too early for the funeral. I suppose you'd difficulty finding your way?

NORMAN: I'd like to talk to her.

BILLY: She's dead . . . you're too late.

NORMAN: Please son . . . give me a minute with her . . .
(BILLY *stops at the door.* NORMAN *has her hand. He is crying/moaning, saying* 'There love, there, it's all right now, love.' *Sobs.*)

55. INT. HOSPITAL WAITING ROOM. EVENING

BILLY *comes back into the little waiting room. His left hand is tightly closed.* JUNE *is there. He sits.*

BILLY: I've never saw a corpse before. She looked sort of surprised. Strange . . . sort of look on her face. She must have been dead nearly half an hour before I realized.
(*He opens his left hand to reveal her rings.*)
She wants Lorna to have these.

JUNE: I called at the house. Lorna told me. I hope you don't mind . . .

BILLY: He turned up late, and stinking of drink. It's funny, the last thing I heard her saying was 'His bloody dinner's going to be cold again.'

JUNE: That was nice, she was thinking about him at the end.

BILLY: He's in there now . . . all this time, and he waits until she's dead before he tries to talk to her!

JUNE: If I was married to someone all those years, I wouldn't want to come up here and watch them dying for an hour every night.

BILLY: What was your da like?

JUNE: An old man, I never knew him as anything else. I should have been his granddaughter . . . so we never really got anything going.

BILLY: They're the loneliest places in the world, these hospitals. Listen.
(*Silence.*)

JUNE: I've made up my mind, Billy. I went to the house to tell you. (*Pause.*) I'm going to York.

BILLY: They need me . . .

JUNE: I could stay for you and never be certain. Then I'd have four years of my mother, as well as the troubles. Maybe all for nothing.

BILLY: My da's going back to England. His brother's a builder. He's going back to work with him.

JUNE: My mother told me I'd not find many young Christian men like you in England. (*Long pause.*) She'll be fine.

BILLY: You'll come back for holidays?

JUNE: Yes . . . and we can write.

56. EXT. THE ENTRANCE TO THE HOSPITAL. EVENING

BILLY *and* JUNE *approach the Lisburn Road entrance to the hospital.*

BILLY: I'll walk you home.

JUNE: No.
(*She kisses him quickly.*)
I'll send my address.
(*She goes. He watches her for a moment, then turns and walks down the road.*)

57. EXT. THE STREET CORNER. DAY

Shortly after the funeral. BILLY *with* IAN. *Dressed in mourning, both of them.*

BILLY: Thanks for coming.

IAN: I liked your ma. (*Pause.*) Should I give myself up?

BILLY: What for? Fletcher's getting better. He doesn't know it was you, and he's said nothing.

IAN: But he'll think it was all you if he remembers.

BILLY: That's right, and he'll be afraid to walk on the same side of the street as me. I'll see you later.

58. INT. THE MARTINS' LIVING ROOM. DAY

BILLY *is sitting.* LORNA, ANN *and* MAUREEN *are standing. Norman's two suitcases are sitting on the floor.* LORNA *is holding a package that contains sandwiches.* NORMAN *comes down the stairs. He wears a suit and is carrying an overcoat, which he now puts on. Checks his hair in the mirror.*

NORMAN: That's it . . . all set.
(*Pause.*)

LORNA: I've made you a few sandwiches.

ANN: Will you write to me, Da?

MAUREEN: And me . . .

NORMAN: In the name of Jasus . . . I'm going over there to work, not to write letters. (*Pause.*) I'll write to Lorna.

LORNA: Have you a clean hankie?

NORMAN: Aye. (*Ill at ease. Pause.*) You two young ones now, be good. I don't want any bad reports. Watch your school and all. Right.

(*He goes awkwardly and kisses* ANN *and* MAUREEN.)

ANN: You be careful, Da.

NORMAN: I'll be fine.

(BILLY *rises and picks up one of the cases.* LORNA *hands* NORMAN *the sandwiches, and they kiss.*)

BILLY: (*Gesturing to the case*) I know you're going to work on a building site, but you don't have to bring your own bricks.

NORMAN: Here . . . you take this one, it's not too bad.

BILLY: (*Moving to the door*) Naw, it's all right.

NORMAN: Wait a minute.

(*He opens the case he carries and squeezes the sandwiches in.*)

LORNA: They'll not be worth eating by the time you've done.

NORMAN: What's in them?

LORNA: Some chicken paste, and some cheese. There's a few buns too.

MAUREEN: Just say the boat sinks?

NORMAN: I'll thumb a lift in a submarine. Right . . . (*To* BILLY) Are you ready?

(BILLY *nods.*)

LORNA: Scribble a wee note as soon as you're there and let us know you're safe, won't you?

NORMAN: Aye . . . aye . . .

(*They go.* NORMAN *kisses* LORNA *at the door.*)

59. EXT. THE STREET. DAY

NORMAN *and* BILLY *walking down the street.* LORNA, ANN *and* MAUREEN *stand at the front watching. Half-way down* NORMAN *turns for a last wave, but the two younger girls are already playing a game.* LORNA *waves. They turn again.* LORNA *goes back into the house.*

60. INT. THE MARTINS' LIVING ROOM. DAY

LORNA *tidying up after Norman's departure.*

61. INT. CITY CENTRE. DAY

NORMAN *and* BILLY *walking towards the P&O terminal.*

62. INT. THE MARTINS' LIVING ROOM. DAY

LORNA *still clearing up.* MAUREEN *and* ANN *come in.*

63. INT. THE FERRY TERMINAL. DAY

The P&O ferry terminal at Belfast Harbour.

BILLY: You'd better go that was the last call.
(*Puts out his hand.*)

NORMAN: (*Taking* BILLY*'s hand*) Yesterday under that coffin's the first time we've had our arms round each other since you were two or three.

BILLY: Stay off the drink, Da.

NORMAN: We made a right pig's arse of it, me and your mother. (*Pause.*) Take care of them for me, son. (*Pause.*) This is the best way.

BILLY: The only way.
(NORMAN *moves as if to embrace him.* BILLY *takes a half-step back.*)
Good luck, Da.
(*They part.*)

64. INT. THE MARTINS' LIVING ROOM. EVENING

ANN *doing dishes.* LORNA *putting* MAUREEN *into her pyjamas. TV on.*

65. INT. THE P&O TERMINAL. EVENING

NORMAN *boarding boat.*

66. EXT. QUEEN ELIZABETH BRIDGE. EVENING

BILLY *on the Queen Elizabeth Bridge gazing at the boat.*

67. INT. THE MARTINS' LIVING ROOM. EVENING

LORNA, *with* ANN, *watching TV.* MAUREEN *asleep.*

68. EXT. THE P&O TERMINAL. EVENING

NORMAN *standing gazing from the boat rail.*

69. EXT. CITY HALL. EVENING

BILLY *passing the City Hall.*

70. INT. THE MARTINS' LIVING ROOM. EVENING

ANN *saying goodnight to* LORNA.

71. EXT. BELFAST CASTLE. EVENING

The boat almost out of sight up the lough.

72. EXT. STREET CORNER. EVENING

BILLY *passing the deserted corner.*

73. INT. THE MARTINS' LIVING ROOM. EVENING

BILLY *enters. He looks at* LORNA *for a moment. She is holding her parents' framed wedding photograph, about to put it away. The others have gone to bed. He takes the photograph from her, looks at it and sets it on the mantelshelf. For the first time in many years.*

LORNA: Are you going to leave it there?

BILLY: That's where it belongs. It's the only way we can all be together in this house.

LORNA: Maureen'll wonder who they are. (*Pause.*) He left me some money, and said he'd send some. (*Pause.*) Did he get away all right?

BILLY: The boat sailed . . . (*Pause. Close-up on wedding photograph.*) That day in the hospital . . . the day she died . . . I thought he was singing to her . . . but he was crying . . . like a dog whining.

LORNA: He used to sing to her, do you remember?

BILLY: She used to sing all the time, when she was cooking anything . . . (*Pause*) . . . then she stopped.

A MATTER OF CHOICE FOR BILLY

Characters

BILLY
LORNA
ANN
MAUREEN
UNCLE ANDY
PAULINE MAGILL
JOHN FLETCHER
IAN
VALERIE AGNEW
SHIRLEY
JOAN
CYRIL WILSON
JUNE
NORMAN

A Matter of Choice for Billy was first shown on BBC Television on 10 May 1983. The cast was as follows:

BILLY	Kenneth Branagh
LORNA	Brid Brennan
ANN	Tracey Lynch
MAUREEN	Aine Gorman
UNCLE ANDY	Mark Mulholland
PAULINE MAGILL	Julia Dearden
JOHN FLETCHER	John Hewitt
IAN	Colum Convey
VALERIE AGNEW	Anne McCartney
SHIRLEY	Chrissie Cotterill
JOAN	Deirdre Morgan
CYRIL WILSON	Nigel Anthony
JUNE	Mary Jackson
NORMAN	James Ellis
Producers	Neil Zeiger and Chris Parr
Director	Paul Seed
Designer	Diane Menaul

1. EXT. THE BOTTOM OF THE STREET. NIGHT

The corner of the butcher's shop. IAN *emerges, cautiously, from the entry. He looks carefully up and down the street, then walks slowly, whistling, to the corner. He stands, casual, giving the impression he's been there a long time. After a moment* VALERIE AGNEW *emerges from the street below and walks towards him.*

IAN: All right . . . nobody see you?

VALERIE: This is stupid . . . I'd like to know why we're still hiding.

IAN: Keep it down, anybody could come along. You walk on up . . . I'll wait a wee while.

VALERIE: (*Agitated*) For goodness' sake . . .

(*She walks quickly away, agitated.*)

2. INT. THE MARTINS' LIVING ROOM. NIGHT

Their parents' wedding photograph is on the fireplace. The fire is lit. LORNA *and* ANN *are sitting.*

ANN: I think you should go out there . . . he must have fell down the hole.

LORNA: Don't be crude.

ANN: It shouldn't take anybody this long to go to the toilet.

LORNA: Just give over . . . don't embarrass him any more.

ANN: I haven't embarrassed him.

(*Sound of the loo flushing.*)

Here he comes at last.

(JOHN FLETCHER *comes in through the back. Washes his hands at the sink and enters the living room.*)

JOHN: (*Rather pale*) I think I'll go on . . . (*Putting on his coat*) I'll see you tomorrow.

(LORNA *goes with him to the door.*)

Goodnight, Ann.

ANN: Goodnight, John.

LORNA: (*Leaving the inner door open, from the hallway*) Goodnight, love.

ANN: (*Smirking as* LORNA *re-enters*) 'Goodnight, love' . . . this sounds serious.

LORNA: Give over.

ANN: He's changed you know, John Fletcher. I never used to like him . . . but he's better since our Billy kicked his head in.

LORNA: That's enough . . . you keep quiet about that.

3. EXT. THE TOP OF THE STREET. NIGHT

A car is sitting. BILLY *emerges from the passenger side. He walks around behind it to the driver's side, and kisses* PAULINE *through the window.* PAULINE *is a young, newly qualified nurse, turned 22.*

BILLY: I'll see you tomorrow night then?

PAULINE: Fine . . . 'night.

BILLY: 'Night, Pauline.

(*He stands and watches as she drives off, then turns slowly towards the street.*)

4. INT. HOSPITAL SIDE-WARD. NIGHT

UNCLE ANDY *lies sleeping. A* NURSE *comes in. She checks the chart on the end of the bed, then starts to tuck in the bedclothes. He grunts and turns over. She goes to his locker . . . takes a grape . . . opens a box of chocolates . . . takes a moment to select one. She leaves, turning the light out as she goes. Pause on* ANDY.

5. EXT. STREET. NIGHT

IAN *watches* FLETCHER *disappear down a street on the far side of the road. He turns and starts walking up the street.* BILLY *is on his way down. They meet.*

IAN: Billy.

BILLY: Ian. I was just goin' to have a wee look up the road before I go in.

IAN: It's dead quiet . . . nobody about.

BILLY: I thought I saw you talking to somebody when I was coming down.

IAN: Aye, Fletcher. The oul tummy's playing him up, he near had to run home.

BILLY: Where's Shirley?

IAN: (*Uneasy*) Dunno, sure we're still narking.

BILLY: This final or what?

IAN: Dunno . . . I still see her . . . just letting her know she's not married to me yet.

BILLY: What's this I hear about you and wee Valerie Agnew?

IAN: (*Very ill at ease*) Aye . . . ah that's nothing.

BILLY: That's not what I heard . . . I heard she's blew Shirley out.

IAN: (*Nervous laugh*) Blew Shirley out . . . that'll be the day. (*Quickly*) What about your new girl?

BILLY: Which one?

IAN: Aye now you're talking . . . play the field, best way, what?

BILLY: Depends how big your field is mate . . . (*smiling*) what? (*They turn and start walking up the street together. They reach Billy's house.*)

IAN: I'll see you the morra, Billy.

BILLY: (*As* IAN *walks on, relieved to get away*) Aye . . . see you.

6. INT. PAULINE'S FLAT. NIGHT

PAULINE *is in her dressing-gown. She picks up a photograph of* BILLY *and pins it on the wall, underneath a large map of North America. She gazes at the photo. Then runs a finger over the map. She appears slightly perplexed.*

7. EXT. THE STREET/THE MARTINS' LIVING ROOM. NIGHT

BILLY *putting bottles on the window sill. He re-enters the house, locking the door.* LORNA *and* ANN *emerge from the scullery and serve up tea and toast.*

BILLY: (*To* ANN) You're up late.

ANN: I can't sleep if I go to bed early. Were you out with Pauline?

BILLY: Yes . . . we just went for a drive.

ANN: Lorna says Uncle Andy's coming here on Tuesday.

BILLY: (*Good-natured, with a glance to* LORNA) Welcome to the elders of the tribe.

LORNA: It's not a secret . . . and it's not as if she mightn't notice him.

ANN: How long will he be here, Billy?

BILLY: Probably a week or so.

LORNA: I hope it's only a week. I wasn't even asked before it was arranged.

BILLY: I've explained that. Come on now . . . he's an old man and we're all he has.

LORNA: There was a time he was nearly all *we* had . . . but he never did much for us.

BILLY: He helped me the time my da threw me out.

LORNA: He only did that because he hates Dad.

ANN: Should we not write and ask my da?

LORNA: I know what the answer would be.

BILLY: My da's away . . . we run the house now.

ANN: My da'd tell him to get stuffed.

LORNA: He's a filthy old brute too . . . spitting into the fire, it turns my stomach.

BILLY: It's only a habit.

LORNA: He's got a dozen habits and they're all filthy. We don't get on, you know that. The day of Mum's funeral he sat there moaning that I'd only put the skin of the tomatoes into his sandwiches. I was confronted in front of everybody. If it hadn't been out of respect for Mum I'd have smashed the plate over his head.

ANN: I 'member he got drunk that day and my da near hit him . . . (*To* BILLY) our Maureen had to run out for you . . . do you remember that, Lorna?

LORNA: (*Quietly*) Yes.

8. INT. THE MARTINS' LIVING ROOM. DAY

Flashback. The day of Janet's funeral. ANDY *is sitting drinking and smoking.* ANN *and* MAUREEN *are sitting.* LORNA *is tidying up. She brings dishes into the scullery.* NORMAN *is there, reflective, smoking.*

LORNA: Are you all right, Dad?

NORMAN: (*Emotional*) 'Course I'm all right. (*Pause.*) It was for the best, love, wasn't it?

LORNA: Of course, Dad . . . she's happy now . . . no more pain.

NORMAN: Aye . . . it's all over for her now. (*Pause.*) It was a good turn out, wasn't it?
(*He wipes his eyes.*)

LORNA: It was great, Dad . . . come on . . . away out to the fire.

NORMAN: I don't want to go out and sit with that oul shite. Has he no bloody home to go to?

LORNA: He sounds drunk.

NORMAN: He must only ate at funerals too.

ANDY: The man himself . . . where'd you get to? I was beginning to think maybe we'd buried you by mistake. Do you want a beer?

NORMAN: Naw . . . I'm all right.

ANDY: You lost a good woman the day . . . I hope you realize that.

NORMAN: I know she was a good woman, it doesn't need you to tell me that.

ANDY: Aye, well mind you you'll miss her now. She was one good girl, our Janet . . . one good girl.
(MAUREEN *sniffs.*)
Poor childer've lost their mother . . . them's who I feel sorry for.

NORMAN: Lorna's looked after them for years, they'll be all right.

ANDY: Not the same . . . a sister's a sister, but your mother's always your mother I always say. Our Janet was a good mother to them youngsters. Now you can't take that away from her.

NORMAN: I'm trying to take nothing away from her.

ANDY: She might be dead and gone now . . . but I'll spake up for her.

NORMAN: I'm saying nothing about her.

ANDY: I know the sort of things went on here at times . . . I'm no oul mug.

NORMAN: What are you talking about?

LORNA: (*Anxious*) Uncle Andy, I think you should think about going . . . before it gets dark.

ANDY: Dark or no dark, she was a good woman's all I'm saying.

NORMAN: Now listen you . . . if you've something to say to me you get it off your chest now . . . pure and clear, no bating about the bush.

LORNA: (*Concerned*) Maureen, away out and tell Billy I want him . . . quick.

ANDY: (*As* MAUREEN *goes*) No point buying flowers after somebody's dead, there was no roses when she was here.

NORMAN: What the hell do you know about what was here . . . when did you ever bother with her?

ANDY: Me and Janet was always very close.

NORMAN: Very close my arse . . .

LORNA: Dad . . . come on, this isn't very nice and Mum just gone.

ANDY: Just gone, and God love her, she's happier now than she ever was here.

NORMAN: (*Rising angrily and knocking* ANDY*'s drink over the floor*) Get up and get to hell out of my house.

ANDY: (*Struggling to his feet*) In the name of Jasus . . . what'd you spill the bloody drink for?

NORMAN: If you don't get out of my house it's your bloody blood I'll spill.

ANDY: (*As* BILLY *enters*) Oh, is that so . . . are you going to bate me the way you bate her . . . and your own son there.

LORNA: (*Holding on to* NORMAN) Don't listen to him, Dad.

BILLY: What's going on?

NORMAN: (*Straining to control himself, quietly*) Take him away, son . . . take him away or I'll swing for him.

ANN: (*Bounding up the stairs*) I'll get his coat.

ANDY: Here, just a minute . . .

BILLY: I'll walk over with you, Uncle Andy.

LORNA: Sit down, Dad, and I'll make you a cup of tea.

(NORMAN *slumps into a chair and lights a cigarette.*)

ANDY: (*As* ANN *appears with his coat*) He should save his energy for the building sites of Birmingham. It's all very well . . .

BILLY: Uncle Andy, shut up and put this coat on.

(ANDY *does so sullenly and leaves with* BILLY. *Hold on* LORNA *and* NORMAN. *She sits and puts a hand on his shoulder.*)

9. INT. THE MARTINS' LIVING ROOM. NIGHT

Back in the present.

ANN: If my da finds out he might come over and kick him out.

BILLY: It's time you were in bed, come on.

ANN: I haven't finished my tea.

BILLY: Hurry up, it's late . . . (*Pause.*) Move it.

ANN: For goodness' sake . . . see the people in this house. I'll not be able to sleep if I get indigestion from rushing.

(ANN *finishes her tea and goes, goodnights said, etc.*)

LORNA: Do you want more tea?

BILLY: Aye, not so much sugar this time.

(*She goes and fetches it.*)

LORNA: How's Pauline?

BILLY: She's fine.

LORNA: Are you going to bring her round?

BILLY: Yea, some night.

LORNA: Is she still talking about going away?

BILLY: Aye . . . it's up to her, isn't it?

LORNA: How many are you going to let walk away, Billy? I didn't want you to go with June . . . but we could manage now . . . if it's just us.

BILLY: There's Uncle Andy now.

LORNA: That's only for a week, isn't it? (*Pause.*) Billy?

BILLY: I think it'll be more than a week . . . how much more probably depends on you.

LORNA: For goodness' sake . . . why wasn't I even asked?

BILLY: I just got worried about him after the last attack. I mean it was just a fluke I went over that night. He could still be lying there, and he'd have died.

LORNA: I'll have to mention it to Dad . . . he'll not be pleased.

BILLY: Look, he doesn't want to come here any more than you want him to. Let's wait and see . . . I mean he might be all right. (*Pause.*)

LORNA: John and me's going to the pictures on Monday night.

BILLY: (*Rising*) It's time I was in my bed.

LORNA: Billy . . . he's all right. You could be a bit friendlier.

BILLY: You'd better get somebody to look after the young ones.

LORNA: (*Annoyed, picking up his cup*) I know . . .

(*She goes into the scullery and starts clearing up. He goes quietly to bed.*)

10. INT. HOSPITAL. THE SIDE-WARD. DAY

ANDY *is shaving, the basin, mirror etc., on the shelf of his bedside locker. Nurse* PAULINE MAGILL *comes in.*

PAULINE: Good afternoon, Mr Morrison, and how are we today?

ANDY: I'm bloody awful, you'll have to speak for yourself.

PAULINE: Oh dear, old grump again. Come on, Mr Morrison, you should be happy. Sure you're going home in a couple of days.

ANDY: I'm not going home. I'm goin' into lodgin's. (*Pause.*) Could I have clean water to rinse my face? (*He combs his hair.* PAULINE *draws water from the sink in the side-ward.*)

PAULINE: The trouble you go to for those girls, I hope they appreciate it. Sister says after the visitors are gone we've to dress you and sit you out in a chair. Later on we'll walk you up the ward. Would you like that?

ANDY: (*Flatly*) I can barely wait. Walk me down the corridor. I don't want to listen to the yapping and gerning of that lot in there. They're like a lot of oul women.

PAULINE: They're all very fond of you. Sammy's upset because you don't play him draughts any more.

ANDY: That's an oul woman's game.

PAULINE: He thinks it's because he beat you last time.

ANDY: Bate me! Sure he chated like hell. When I went for a pee he give himself more crowners than the Royal Family has.

PAULINE: What'll you do when you're out? Do you play bowls?

ANDY: (*With contempt*) No, I do not. That's a game for randy geriatrics.

PAULINE: Honestly . . . I don't know what we're going to do with you. What do you play?

ANDY: Russian roulette's my game . . . but I've run out of partners for the minute. (*Pause. He finishes off.*) Is Billy coming up this afternoon?

PAULINE: I don't know, I don't think so. Didn't he say?

ANDY: He's more liable to tell his plans to you than me.

PAULINE: He didn't say he'd be up today.

ANDY: You realize he's just lost his mother?

PAULINE: His mother! Yes, about a year ago, I know.

ANDY: Young fella like him can get daft notions after a shock like that.

PAULINE: Mr Morrison, whatever else I am, I don't see myself as a substitute mother. Billy and me are just friends.

ANDY: Friends, aye . . . it takes a while to get over the likes of that's all I'm saying. (*As she goes*) Give me over that paper before you go.

11. INT. THE MARTINS' LIVING ROOM. DAY

ANN and MAUREEN *are polishing* BILLY*'s shoes. He is in the scullery shaving. He emerges, half done.*

BILLY: You'll be polishing them shoes away before you're done.

ANN: Mine's the cleanest.

MAUREEN: No, it's not, sure, it's not, Billy?

BILLY: They're both great. If you two were in the army you'd win prizes.

(*He returns to his shaving so that they have to raise their voices.*)

MAUREEN: Uncle Andy was in the army, wasn't he, Billy?

BILLY: Aye . . . according to him he was the army.

MAUREEN: He used to be in the jungle.

ANN: He says he got medals for killing thousands of Japs.

MAUREEN: He was going to marry a Japanese princess once.

ANN: I don't believe that. What would a Japanese princess have been doing in the jungle? Wise it. Do you believe that, Billy?

BILLY: (*Emerging, drying his face*) Sometimes he exaggerates a bit.

MAUREEN: What does that mean?

ANN: It means he tells lies.

MAUREEN: He does not . . . he showed me her picture.

ANN: He probably found that . . . or took it from one of them Japs he killed . . . he's an oul cod.

MAUREEN: I'm goin' to tell him on you.

ANN: I don't care.

MAUREEN: I'll tell him you said he was a liar.

ANN: Tell him, he probably knows he is anyway.

BILLY: Girls, girls . . . that's enough.

12. EXT. STREET. DAY

IAN *and* VALERIE *looking through the window of H. Samuel's. They are inspecting the engagement rings.*

VALERIE: Oh, look at that one . . . the big cluster . . . I'd love that.

IAN: You'd need a big cluster of money for that . . . we don't want to go mad.

VALERIE: That's just bloody typical. Oul skinflint, I must be mad for getting engaged to the likes of you.

IAN: Will we go and see what they have inside?

VALERIE: You mean the cheap ones? It's not bloody Shirley you're marrying you know. Why don't we just go to a hardware shop and buy a brass curtain ring and have done with it?

(*She prances off into the shop and leaves him standing. He follows.*)

IAN: Ah . . . love . . . don't be like that about it . . . come 'ere.

13. INT. THE MARTINS' LIVING ROOM. DAY

ANN *and* MAUREEN *playing ludo.* BILLY *comes downstairs dressed. The girls look at him and giggle as he combs his hair.*

BILLY: What's so funny?

(*The girls continue to giggle.*)

MAUREEN: Are you going out with Pauline, Billy?

BILLY: No . . . I'm going down the town with Ian.

(*They just giggle as he glares at them.*)

ANN: Maureen! It's her, Billy, she's making me laugh.

(LORNA *and* JOHN *enter, carrying bags of groceries. When* JOHN *has left his stuff in the scullery he returns and stands awkwardly.*)

JOHN: What about you, Billy? That's not a bad oul day.

BILLY: Aye, it's all right.

LORNA: (*Coming in from the scullery and removing her coat*) Sit down, John, I have the teapot on.

JOHN: Ah no . . . look . . . I'll . . .

(*Pause.* LORNA *catches* BILLY*'s eye.*)

BILLY: Sit down for a minute sure.

JOHN: (*Sitting with hesitation*) Aye, well just for a minute . . . (*takes out cigarette, offering*) Billy. . . ?

BILLY: No, I don't use them, thanks.

JOHN: Wise man . . . do you mind. . . ?

BILLY: Sure, go ahead.

ANN: Smoking's bad for you, John.

JOHN: (*Self-conscious*) Aye, I know, love.

MAUREEN: It gives you brown stains on your teeth . . .

ANN: And when you kiss our Lorna your breath'll be bad.

(MAUREEN *and* ANN *giggle.*)

BILLY: That's enough you two . . . just behave.

14. EXT. CORNER. DAY

SHIRLEY *is standing.* IAN *comes and stands, not seeing her until he's already there. She stiffens. They stand looking in opposite directions. He glances at her. Then pretends to just notice her.*

IAN: Shirley . . . what about you? I didn't notice you there.

(*She looks him up and down with contempt, then turns away again.*)

That's a right day.

SHIRLEY: (*Icily*) Are you talking to me? Because if you are I don't hear you.

IAN: I was just saying hello.

SHIRLEY: Shove your hellos up your arse. (*Pause.*) And another thing . . . if you've anything to say to me, the first thing you've to say is to apologize.

IAN: I ah . . . I suppose you've heard about me and Valerie.

SHIRLEY: She's been with that many, it's probably just your turn. (*With scorn*) She must be getting desperate . . . huh, I wouldn't be surprised you'll be getting engaged next.

IAN: Well ah . . .

SHIRLEY: (*Taking a step away*) I've told you . . . when you want to talk to me again, start with apologizing.

(*She walks away.* IAN *motions as if to speak again, but doesn't as he watches her walk away. He looks miserable.*)

15. INT. THE SIDE-WARD. DAY

LORNA, ANN, MAUREEN *and* JOHN *are there with* ANDY. ANDY *nurses a couple of brown envelopes.*

LORNA: (*Uneasy*) I watered your plants.

ANDY: Did you make sure you locked up well after you?

LORNA: Of course I did.

ANN: I thought you said you thought you left the back door open?

LORNA: Ann, give over.

ANDY: I wouldn't be surprised at that. (*Holding up the envelopes*) Coming up to a sick man with a fistful of bills.

LORNA: You told me to bring the mail and them's all there was. It's not my fault.

ANDY: You might have knowed I didn't mean bills. In the name of Jasus.

ANN: You shouldn't swear like that in front of our Maureen.

ANDY: I hope you didn't leave any lights burning? The electric's dear enough. If they'd make them Fenian gets pay their way.

ANN: (*Plucking another grape, the latest of many*) Uncle Andy, you're always gerning.

ANDY: Never you mind your oul cheek, young madam.

ANN: Our Lorna goes over and cleans your oul house and all you ever do's yap.

ANDY: I'm a sick man.

MAUREEN: (*Matter-of-factly*) You make me sick listening to you. My da used to say you'd the face gerned off yourself. (*Pause.*) Give's another one Ann. (*Grape.*)

LORNA: Ann, that's enough. They're Uncle Andy's.

ANDY: Let the childer tear away. They're only grapes.

ANN: (*Holding up the almost bare twig*) You can always carve boats with your penknife. The way you did when you were a prisoner of war.

16. INT. THE MARTINS' LIVING ROOM. DAY

BILLY *is there. The door raps and* IAN *enters.*

IAN: What about you?

BILLY: What kept you?

IAN: Ah, sure it's time enough. Where're the rest?

BILLY: Hospital. (*Rising*) Are you right?

IAN: Ah. Just. Could I have a word with you . . . Private like?
(*Both sit.*)
I'm getting married.

BILLY: Married! (*Pause.*) What do you want to get married for?

IAN: I have to. Valerie's pregnant.
(BILLY *laughs. After a moment they are both laughing and take a while to recover.*)

BILLY: Valerie Agnew. How did it happen?

IAN: How? Well like . . . You know, we had that intercourse thing.

BILLY: I didn't think she was the Virgin Mary. How far is she?

IAN: Three months or so. We got engaged this morning.

BILLY: You kept quiet long enough.

IAN: I wanted to be sure. Make sure I couldn't say no before I said yes.

BILLY: What did her da say?

IAN: He got me by the throat. I'd have dropped him but you can't hit your own kid's granda.

BILLY: What about Shirley?

IAN: She doesn't know. I tried till explain. She thought I was trying to get going with her again and stormed off.

BILLY: You and Shirley's been going together since we were in primary school.

IAN: I know. I didn't mean it. I mean I liked Shirley. I was just looking at her. . . .

BILLY: Behave yourself. You're almost a married man. Valerie's all right. (*Pause.*) Not bad.

IAN: (*Solemn*) I wasn't the first you know.

BILLY: Start worrying if you're not the last. When's the big day?

IAN: As soon as possible. Before the neighbours start to notice.

BILLY: Most of them can count to ten.

IAN: I'm going down till the registry office on Monday . . . make the arrangements.

BILLY: I thought it would have been the cathedral, all white, a hundred guests, and a honeymoon in the Bahamas?

IAN: You're close. The City Hall, only ma's and da's. And a honeymoon in Bangor. (*Pause.*) I was hoping like . . . you'd be best man.

BILLY: (*Rising*) You know me. Anything for a laugh.

17. INT. THE SIDE-WARD. DAY

As Scene 15.

ANDY: (*To* JOHN) Here, give's another one of them fags.

LORNA: (*As* JOHN *does*) Uncle Andy, you shouldn't. (*To* JOHN) And you shouldn't encourage him. You should be ashamed.

ANDY: You know, I think the ability till nag is born with a woman.

LORNA: What's the point of the doctor's treating your chest if you're going to go on smoking?

ANDY: Treating me arse. Them fellas couldn't treat a tea chest for woodworm.

ANN: What age were you when you started smoking, Uncle Andy?

ANDY: From the age of five I used to take a wee puff of my da's pipe.

MAUREEN: Is that why you're so small?

ANDY: I've always been as big as I needed to be. (*Pause.*) Tell that other fella till bring me up a bottle of stout the night.

LORNA: I will not indeed. You're not allowed to drink and smoke in hospitals.

ANDY: If you're allowed till die in them, I don't see how they can object to anything else.

18. EXT. THE CORNER. DAY

SHIRLEY *and* JOAN *at the corner.*

SHIRLEY: (*Shaken but trying not to show*) Who told you that?

JOAN: I saw it.

SHIRLEY: I was talking to him here a while ago, he never said anything.

JOAN: (*Wetting her finger and crossing her heart*) I swear to God, cross my heart and hope to die.

SHIRLEY: How do you know? What finger was it on?

JOAN: (*Showing the appropriate finger*) That one . . . they're engaged. It's gorgeous. A big cluster.

SHIRLEY: (*Furious and hurt*) Wait till I see him. (*Clenching her fist*) I'll give him a big cluster right across the bake.

19. INT. A BAR. AFTERNOON

BILLY *and* IAN *are having a pint.*

IAN: There's another wee thing. (*Pause.*) I'm thinking of going intil business. If you're interested.

BILLY: What as . . . a stud?

IAN: Winda cleaning. I'm buying a ladder. (*Pause.*) There could be a partnership if you want.

BILLY: You mean you want half the money for the ladders?

IAN: No, Valerie's oul fella's looking after that.

BILLY: (*Uninterested*) I've got a job.

IAN: You could work with me at weekends and nights. Few extra bob.

BILLY: Are you buying two ladders?

IAN: You could use a chair. Do the downstairs.

BILLY: Catch yourself on.

IAN: No, serious. An oul chair and up on the windy sills.

BILLY: I can just see me tramping round the streets with a chair.

IAN: I'm offering. Favour for a mate, but if you're not interested. Think about it.
(*Pause.*)

BILLY: I've thought about it, I can earn more labouring where I am. Are you going to live in her house?

IAN: Wise up. We've got a flat.
(BILLY *looks at him.*)
Her da got it. It needs doing up, but it's all right. Down Botanic Avenue. Close to the railway station. Handy that.

BILLY: Why? Are you going to wipe the train windies as they pass through?

IAN: You can laugh mate, but I'm going to do all right. Her da's it all worked out.

BILLY: He'll probably give you a list of positions for the honeymoon.

IAN: Huh, I could show him one or two.

BILLY: It's a pity you hadn't known how to reverse.
(*Pause*)

IAN: What about this girl of yours then? Is this the big one?

BILLY: She's about five foot five or six. Just because you've caught cold doesn't mean I've got to sneeze in sympathy.

IAN: Have you? You know . . . got it yet?

BILLY: What do you think?

IAN: What about Lorna and Fletcher then?
(BILLY *glares at him.*)
No . . . no, I didn't mean . . .
(*Hold on* BILLY—*thinking.*)

20. INT. THE MARTINS' LIVING ROOM. MORNING

LORNA *getting* MAUREEN *ready for school.* ANN *is reading a letter*

ANN: (*Related to letter, tearful*) Is he going to marry her?

LORNA: You know as much as I do. Will you hurry up. You're going to be late.

ANN: (*Replacing letter in envelope and placing it on the mantelpiece*) I hate school on Mondays.

MAUREEN: I hate school every day.

LORNA: Run on. It'll not be so bad when you get into it.

ANN: I've a sore stomach.

LORNA: (*Herding her out through the door*) Go on, and straight home. I want the dinner over early. I'm going to the pictures.

MAUREEN: Who's looking after us?

LORNA: Ian and Valerie.

MAUREEN: What about Shirley?

LORNA: Never mind that now.

MAUREEN: Why do they have to come in? We're not babies you know.

LORNA: Well stop acting like it and get ready for school. Have you got that hair combed yet?

21. INT. HEADMASTER'S OFFICE. DAY

CYRIL WATSON *there. A knock on the door.*

CYRIL: (*Calls*) Come in.

(ANN *enters sheepishly, crosses and stands by his desk.*)

Ann Martin?

(*She nods.*)

ANN: (*Mutters*) Yes.

CYRIL: (*Glancing at her file*) Miss Semple has told me about your little episode, madam. What have you to say for yourself?

ANN: Nothing, sir . . . I'm sorry . . . I lost my temper.

CYRIL: Indeed, well now I'm going to lose mine. Miss Semple is one of my most conscientious teachers . . . a lady. She doesn't have to take abuse from a young guttersnipe like you. (*Reading*) If I'd been here on Friday afternoon . . . (*Pause.*) You live with your brother and sister?

ANN: Yes, sir.

CYRIL: Stand still, girl. Your father's away in England, is that correct?

ANN: Yes, sir.

CYRIL: Mother deceased . . . correct?

ANN: Yes, sir.

CYRIL: Have you told your brother and sister about this little escapade?

ANN: No, sir.

CYRIL: Oh, you haven't . . . not important, didn't you think?

ANN: No, sir, I mean, sir . . .

CYRIL: Maybe you're not being properly controlled at home?

ANN: Yes, sir, I am, sir . . . honestly, sir.

CYRIL: Will you stand still. It's high time some of you young thugs were taught a short, sharp lesson in obedience. My staff should not . . . and indeed they do not have to take abuse from the likes of you. Is that clear?

ANN: Yes, sir . . . It'll never happen again, sir.

CYRIL: No, well I'm going to ensure that it doesn't, Martin. I'm going to suspend you, starting right away. You'll go home . . .

(ANN *starts to cry.*)

. . . and on Friday morning you'll return here with your older sister. I'll decide then whether I want you back in my school. Is that clear?

(ANN *can't answer.*)

Is that clear?

ANN: Yes, sir.

CYRIL: Stop crying . . . your tears are lost on me. Go and collect your belongings and be off the school premises immediately . . . until half-past ten on Friday morning.

ANN: (*Sobbing*) Please, sir . . .

CYRIL: Go . . . now, before I expel you on the spot.

(ANN *goes.*)

22. EXT. THE TOP CORNER. DAY

Much later in the day. ANN *and* JOAN *are there.*

ANN: Friday at half-past ten.

JOAN: You're lucky . . . I wish he'd suspend me. My ma'd get me a job.

ANN: Our Billy'll kill me if he finds out. Lorna near hit the roof.

JOAN: What for? Sure oul Watson's only an oul perfert. 'Toucher' the boys call him.

ANN: He could get us put away in the home . . . that's what our Lorna says.

JOAN: Your Billy'd kick his head in if he did . . . he wouldn't dare. (*Lighting up a cigarette end*) Do you want a puff?

ANN: No . . . I'm in trouble enough.

JOAN: I suppose your Billy doesn't allow you? (*Pause.*) Will you be at the corner tonight?

ANN: No, Lorna's going out.

JOAN: I'm going to lumber Shugie tonight.

ANN: Are you . . . I thought he was dirty?

JOAN: He kisses like a film star and his hands are everywhere.

ANN: Our Billy'd kill me if I lumbered anybody.

JOAN: Why, what does your Billy do with his girls?

ANN: I don't know.

JOAN: I'll bet you he does a lot more than just kiss them. He's lovely looking your Billy.

(ANN *shows no interest in continuing the conversation.*)

I'd better go down and do the dishes before my ma comes

home. I'll maybe see you later.

ANN: See you.

(ANN *watches her go down the street and reluctantly follows.*)

23. INT. THE SIDE-WARD. DAY

ANDY *in bed.* BILLY *sitting with him.*

ANDY: What's going on between you and that Nurse Magill one?

BILLY: We're just friends.

ANDY: Oh aye, do you think I'm a bloody fool? Do you know she's a Mick?

BILLY: Look, don't start.

ANDY: Them kinda friends are dangerous, you don't need them.

BILLY: Do you care what she is when she's looking after you?

ANDY: I might like her making the bed, but I don't want her in it beside me.

BILLY: Come on, what about all your exploits?

ANDY: Them was different . . . I was in foreign parts. I wasn't resident in an open-air asylum.

BILLY: Nobody worries about them things now.

ANDY: In the name of Jasus . . . did your da bate you stupid? That's the sort of things they blow your kneecaps off for . . . that's if you're lucky. Sure you don't know what her or her ones are involved in.

BILLY: I can look after myself, quit fussing. Remember it's me who's taking you home to look after you.

ANDY: Look after me arse . . . If your da knew he'd swim back across the Irish Sea.

BILLY: My da's got nothing to do with me.

ANDY: Your da's your da. I feel responsible for yous. He'd expect me to keep an eye out. (*Pause.*) Listen, lad, I'm giving you good advice . . . Micks is all right to make your bed in a hospital, or serve you drink in a bar, but . . .

BILLY: (*Rising, irritated*) Look, I'm going . . .

ANDY: The sooner I get up there the better. You lot need a bit of fatherly advice.

BILLY: Aye . . . that'll be new . . . I'll see you tomorrow.

24. INT. THE MARTINS' LIVING ROOM. EVENING

VALERIE, ANN, MAUREEN, IAN *and* JOHN *are there.* LORNA *is upstairs getting changed.*

ANN: Our Lorna must think it's a midnight movie you're going to.

IAN: Some of the lads were asking why you weren't at the club again yesterday, John.

JOHN: I'm finished with that.

IAN: They're expecting you back.

JOHN: I'm through with the UDA.

IAN: Just like that?

JOHN: My dues are paid up, but I'm stopping that . . . I'm leaving.

IAN: You can't just do that. You know the rules . . . if anybody'd tried that in your day you'd have floored them.

JOHN: Times have changed . . . I got into enough trouble through the UDA.

IAN: That had nothing to do with the UDA . . . you got into a row.

JOHN: It was a row about that.

IAN: It had nothing to do with it . . . you were just shouting your mouth off.

VALERIE: (*To* IAN) I don't know what you're slabbering for . . . your UDA days are over.

IAN: What?

VALERIE: What? What? You heard me. There'll be no more club on a Sunday for you.

IAN: Sure your da goes.

VALERIE: Aye, and many's the time my ma's had to scrape his dinner into the bin. It won't happen with me.

IAN: Ah, come on now, love. I'll have to put my foot down on this one.

VALERIE: You can put down whatever the hell you like . . . You're going to be a married man . . . John's got more sense than you.

IAN: We'll see . . . they'll not just let him walk out like that.

JOHN: I'll have a word with Big Davie, him and me's mates.

VALERIE: When you're having a word with him tell him General

Montgomery here's left as well.

IAN: He'll tell him nothing.

JOHN: They'll understand, Ian. After all you're going to have a . . . (*Realizing* ANN *and* MAUREEN *are listening*) In your circumstances.

IAN: Never mind that . . . there's plenty of the lads has . . .
(VALERIE *kicks him.*)
Ouch. (*Angry*) What the hell did you do that for?

VALERIE: There's children listening.

IAN: (*Realizing*) Anyway I'm staying . . . (*Turning on* JOHN *to give vent to his anger*) You're only getting out because you're yella.

JOHN: (*As* LORNA *comes downstairs*) Who are you calling yella?

IAN: You are.

JOHN: (*Pulling off his coat*) Would you like to come outside and say that?

LORNA: John . . . what's going on? Stop that.

IAN: (*Noting* LORNA*'s presence*) Aye certainly . . . (*Going to the door*) Come on . . .

LORNA: That's enough of that . . . your street-fighting days are over, John.

IAN: Come on, big man.

VALERIE: (*To* IAN) You sit down and shut your gub.

JOHN: (*Putting his coat back on*) If it wasn't for Lorna I'd take you out and wipe that street with you.

IAN: Anytime you like . . . mouth.

LORNA: Ian! Are you ready, John?

25. INT. PAULINE'S FLAT. EVENING

BILLY *is in the bed.* PAULINE *is on the telephone in the other room. She hangs up and comes in. She is wearing a dressing-gown and smoking.*

BILLY: Who was it . . . a boyfriend?

PAULINE: My mother . . . wanting to know why I wasn't over for dinner yesterday. See . . . you're even making me neglect my own family.

BILLY: Hurry up and put that cigarette out.

PAULINE: (*Holding it up*) I can't waste all that. I've an interview next Wednesday. For a job in Toronto.

BILLY: I hope you don't get it.

PAULINE: Gee thanks . . . it's in the Europa at seven o'clock.

BILLY: When would you go, if you get it?

PAULINE: I don't know . . . early in the New Year. (*Pause.*) Don't look so gloomy. Maybe I'll not get it . . . knowing my luck probably not.

BILLY: Why bother going for it then?

PAULINE: I have to, Billy. It's been a dream of mine for years . . . I want to get out of this place.

BILLY: Away from me?

PAULINE: (*Moving closer to him, stroking his head with her free hand*) I don't want to leave you . . . you know that.

BILLY: You don't make much sense at times.

PAULINE: I want you to come with me.

BILLY: (*Pushing her hand away, irritated*) I can't, you know that.

PAULINE: Then make me a better offer.

(*Long pause.*)

BILLY: Come on in.

PAULINE: What was your Uncle Andy saying about me?

BILLY: Never mind him.

PAULINE: (*Stubbing her cigarette out*) I do mind . . . would you like a cup of coffee?

BILLY: No, I would not . . . will you come on?

PAULINE: To your Uncle Andy I'm just a wee Fenian . . . to you . . . just do this and then you're away in another half-hour.

BILLY: Ah for . . . (*Pause.*) What do you want me to do?

PAULINE: Stay with me. Come away with me . . . or . . . (*Pause.*) Billy. . . .

(*He pulls her to him and they kiss.*)

26. INT. THE MARTINS' LIVING ROOM. EVENING

IAN, VALERIE, ANN *and* MAUREEN *there.*

ANN: You used to say you'd never get married, Ian.

MAUREEN: Are you making him, Valerie?

VALERIE: Of course . . . I'm taking him before anyone else comes along and grabs him.

ANN: I don't think anyone else would want him.

IAN: Thanks very much . . . cheeky bitch.

MAUREEN: I thought Shirley was the only girl you ever had, Ian. Did she throw you away?

IAN: (*Embarrassed, putting an arm around* VALERIE) This is my true love.

MAUREEN: (*Making a face*) You're easy pleased.

VALERIE: Compliments are flying.

MAUREEN: Our Billy's going with a nurse out of the hospital. She's a you-know-what . . . a Fenian.

ANN: Uncle Andy says he'd give him a good kick up the arse, if he wasn't afraid of causing brain damage.

IAN: Do you like your Uncle Andy?

ANN: You always ask me that, Ian. That's a sign you're going mad . . . when you start repeating yourself.

MAUREEN: Are you going to have a big white dress, Valerie?

VALERIE: No, just a suit.

MAUREEN: I'd hate that. When I get married I'm going to have a big white dress and a dead long veil.

ANN: I'm never going to get married.

27. EXT. COASTAL PATH. EVENING

JOHN *and* LORNA *strolling along the coastal path at Holywood.*

JOHN: Your da'll never approve, will he?

LORNA: I don't know. (*Pause.*) I love the sea. I'd like to live beside it.

JOHN: Down here?

LORNA: No, it's too tame here . . . somewhere more remote . . . where it's wilder.

(*Pause. She's preoccupied with her own thoughts.*)

JOHN: Ian got brave all of a sudden. I remember the time he was afraid to say 'boo' to me.

LORNA: I don't want you to leave things and change just for me. I want you to do what you want to do.

JOHN: I am . . . it's the same thing.

(*They stop and stand in silence gazing out to sea.*)

LORNA: My mother loved the sea. They used to take us down to Bangor . . . I don't really remember it . . . sand, water, but she used to tell me.

JOHN: Your da was bad to her, wasn't he?

LORNA: They loved each other . . . but they just couldn't live together.

JOHN: There used to be a lot of gossip.

LORNA: Yes . . . there was.

(*Pause. She turns and walks on.*)

28. INT. THE MARTINS' LIVING ROOM. EVENING

VALERIE: (*Serving the supper*) Eat all that toast up now, there's plenty of good butter on it.

MAUREEN: You're not supposed to put butter on the toast.

ANN: We always use marge. The butter's for our Billy's piece.

VALERIE: Ach well, it'll not matter just this once.

IAN: I think it's near bedtime when you've finished that, girls.

ANN: I'm going to write a letter to my da.

MAUREEN: My da's got a girlfriend.

ANN: Maureen . . . that's private . . . our Lorna'll kill you.

IAN: (*Laughs.*) Eh, the boul Norman's got a girlfriend.

ANN: (*Sharply*) No, he hasn't, and the last time you called him Norman he bounced your head off that wall and had you crying.

(IAN *shifts, uncomfortable.*)

VALERIE: Are you looking forward to having your Uncle Andy here, girls?

ANN: (*As* MAUREEN *shrugs*) He's good for a laugh.

IAN: I remember going over to see him a few times with Billy. I wonder will he remember me?

VALERIE: How could he forget?

IAN: He used to have a big orange cat, didn't he?

(ANN *and* MAUREEN *giggle.*)

Does he still have it?

MAUREEN: No . . . he says the Chinese restaurant stole it and made puss-puss-pooee out of it.

IAN: Billy used to always cadge a few bob of him. He seemed a right sort. (*Laughs.*) He didn't like your da.

ANN: Ian, you'd better leave my da alone. At least he wasn't like your da . . . he didn't go to the park to look up the wee girls' clothes when they were on the swings.

(IAN *is angry and embarrassed, but says nothing.*)

29. INT. PAULINE'S BEDROOM. EVENING

BILLY *and* PAULINE *sitting on the bed drinking coffee. She is fully dressed, he is stripped to the waist.*

PAULINE: Do you have to go home?

BILLY: Yep. (*Rising to dress*) Lorna'll sit up for me.

PAULINE: You're very close, aren't you?

BILLY: We've had to be.

PAULINE: Are you jealous of this boyfriend, John Fletcher?

BILLY: Don't be daft . . . jealous? She's only my sister.

PAULINE: Your sister, your mother, your mistress . . . the only woman you've ever loved.

BILLY: That's rubbish.

PAULINE: I'd love to get you on your knees, Billy. I'd love to have your strength and you my weakness. I'd love to see what that would do to you. Is there anything you're afraid of?

BILLY: I'm afraid of dying of cancer, like my ma. (*Pause.*) I'm afraid of making all the wrong choices and messing everything up, the way my da did. Why can't we just be friends and not have all this serious stuff?

PAULINE: (*Hurt*) Sorry, I thought what we've just done made it serious. (*Pause.*) Yes . . . we can just be friends. (*Lifting his empty cup and sweeping out of the room*) Pen-pals if I get this job.

30. INT. THE MARTINS' LIVING ROOM. EVENING

IAN: (*Just finishing off a cup of tea*) Any more tea, love?

VALERIE: Get lost you. You weren't even supposed to get that until they came in.

(LORNA *and* JOHN *come in.*)

LORNA: I'm sorry we're late . . . we stopped to have chips.

VALERIE: It's all right . . .

IAN: What was the picture like?

VALERIE: Don't tell me anything about it. Ian's taking me on Thursday.

IAN: Since when?

VALERIE: Since bloody now.

IAN: All right, love . . . don't get excited.

VALERIE: I adore Paul Newman . . . he's gorgeous.

IAN: Paul Newman! Sure he's as grey as a badger.

VALERIE: Don't you dare say a thing about him. Being as grey as a badger isn't as bad as looking like a drowned rat.

IAN: Who looks like a rat?

LORNA: Actually we didn't go to the pictures. We went to Holywood for a stroll by the sea.

JOHN: Look folks, time I was away. 'Night all.

(*Replies as he goes.* LORNA *doesn't see him out.*)

LORNA: Did the girls behave, Valerie?

VALERIE: No problem at all.

IAN: She put Billy's butter on the toast by accident.

LORNA: That doesn't matter.

(*Car drawing up.*)

There's a car, it must be Billy.

IAN: Girl with a car and all, that's all right.

(BILLY *and* PAULINE *enter.*)

BILLY: This is Pauline. (*Pointing, as hands are shaken*) Lorna, Valerie, Ian.

LORNA: I've seen you in the hospital.

VALERIE: (*Holding out her hand*) Do you like my ring, Billy?

BILLY: That's a smasher . . . (*To* IAN) It must have set you back a bob or two.

IAN: It's only money. She'll be weighed down with rings and things when I get this business going.

BILLY: (*To* PAULINE) Did you see it, love?

PAULINE: It's beautiful, congratulations.

IAN: That's the sort of thing you want to get out of this character.

(BILLY *glares at him.*)

What about a wee cup of tea, folks?

BILLY: Are you making it?

(LORNA *sits* PAULINE *down.*)

IAN: Valerie will . . . won't you, love?

BILLY: In her condition? Get away . . . you do it.

VALERIE: (*Sitting down*) Here, I wish it was you I was marrying.

IAN: Are you serious?

BILLY: Of course . . . isn't she going to have your baby? She needs rest and looking after. Go on, we're all gasping.

(IAN *goes.*)

LORNA: The girls'll be raging that they missed you, Pauline . . . you'll have to come and meet them sometime.

PAULINE: Of course . . . I'd love to.

VALERIE: I don't know how you can be a nurse . . . the blood and all . . . and washing round dirty oul men.

BILLY: They're not all like Uncle Andy.

(LORNA *shoots him a glance.*)

VALERIE: Do you go to operations and all?

PAULINE: I have done . . . you get used to it.

VALERIE: Oh, I'd get sick . . .

(IAN *brings the tea in.*)

I really would.

IAN: What's all this about the boul Norman having a girlfriend?

(*Silence.* BILLY *is surprised. He looks at* LORNA.)

LORNA: Who said that?

IAN: It ah . . . it was ah . . . just one of the kids . . . probably a wee joke, Billy.

(*Awkward silence.*)

BILLY: You can't make tea very well either.

LORNA: Are you looking forward to it all now, Valerie?

VALERIE: In a way I am and I'm not. The worst bit was telling my ma and da. Especially my da . . . but he's been really great.

LORNA: I could just imagine my dad if it was me.

IAN: It could be you soon. (*Realizing, embarrassed*) I mean getting married.

VALERIE: I'll tell you what it's like before you do it, Lorna.

(*Pause.*) Would your da come over if you were getting married?

LORNA: Of course he would.

IAN: Best man . . . the boul Norman.

BILLY: (*Sharply*) What's all this 'boul Norman' stuff about?

IAN: No harm meant, Billy . . . it's just an expression.

BILLY: Well just drop it.

IAN: Right mate . . . look, we'd better shift. (*Rising*) You know what they say about pregnant women being out late at night.

VALERIE: No, what do they say?

IAN: (*Puzzled*) What?

VALERIE: Forget it . . . move.

LORNA: Thanks very much, I'll do the same for you sometime. (*They go, goodnights said.*)

PAULINE: He seems to have a knack for putting his foot in it.

BILLY: Someday I'll put my foot in him.

PAULINE: You're too quick tempered . . . he seems harmless.

LORNA: Ach, he's only a bit of an idiot, Ian.

BILLY: What's all this girlfriend nonsense?

PAULINE: I'd better go . . .

LORNA: Don't rush off. I'd a letter this morning . . . it's up there. (BILLY *makes no move.*)

He's going with some English woman. He says he'd like to bring her over to meet us . . . that it might give us notions about a new mother.

BILLY: He could walk on eggs.

PAULINE: Are you all ready for Mr Morrison arriving?

LORNA: As ready as I'll ever be. I suppose you'll be glad to get rid of him?

PAULINE: He's a character. If you like I'll come round now and again and give you a break.

LORNA: That would be marvellous. Sure you can drop round any time, you don't have to wait for Billy.

PAULINE: Are you thinking of getting married yourself?

LORNA: I am not . . . that's just Valerie. John's just a friend really.

BILLY: I hate to break this up girls, but I've to rise early.

PAULINE: So have I. (*Rising*) It was really nice to meet you, Lorna. Maybe we could go out some evening . . . give you a break from the kids and Mr Morrison.

LORNA: That would be really great.

(BILLY *sees her out.* LORNA *clears up. Noise of car driving off.* BILLY *returns.*)

BILLY: What do you think?

LORNA: She's lovely. I'd love to go out with her some night. Maybe you'll be the next one to get married.

BILLY: What's the boul Norman's girlfriend called?

LORNA: (*Handing it to him*) There's the letter . . .

BILLY: I don't want to read it . . . what's her name?

LORNA: Mavis.

BILLY: Huh, Save us, Mavis. What else does he say about her?

LORNA: Why don't you just read the letter for yourself?

BILLY: Pauline's going away you know . . . Canada.

LORNA: Have you asked her to stay? You're so like Dad you know . . . keeping everything bottled up inside. It doesn't make you any less of a man to be able to tell someone how you feel.

BILLY: Suppose you don't know? Marry her, or go with her.

LORNA: Is that what she said?

BILLY: More or less . . . she might settle for me just living with her.

LORNA: So why don't you do that?

BILLY: 'Cause I'm afraid a week after I'd got her I'd discover she's not what I want.

LORNA: I'd love to see you happy, Billy.

BILLY: Aye . . . I'd love to see you seeing me happy.

(*They smile.*)

Come on.

31. INT. THE MARTINS' LIVING ROOM. MORNING

Tuesday morning. BILLY *at breakfast, ready for work.*

LORNA: Will you be straight home?

BILLY: Aye. I'll be going to see Pauline, but I'll not be late.

(*Pause.*) What's for my piece?

LORNA: I've just given you bread and butter and two bananas.

BILLY: Any buns?

LORNA: Ann got you two of those big black currant squares you like.

BILLY: Uncle Andy used to say they were a mixture of dead flies and dried scabs.

LORNA: If he starts any of that talk here . . . (*Pause.*) Billy?

BILLY: What?

LORNA: Our Ann's in a wee bit of trouble at school . . . she's been suspended. (*Pause.*) She swore at a teacher and threw things at her. It's this new headmaster trying to make a name for himself.

BILLY: When did this happen?

LORNA: On Friday, but she was only suspended yesterday . . . I've to go up and see Mr Watson on Friday morning.

BILLY: That stupid wee . . . can she never stay out of trouble?

32. EXT. THE HOSPITAL GROUNDS. DAY

JOHN *carrying* ANDY*'s case to the car.* LORNA *walks with* ANDY.

ANDY: I hope there's a good fire on up here?

LORNA: Of course there is.

ANDY: I'm a sick man, you know. I need looking after.

(LORNA *and* JOHN *exchange a look.*)

JOHN: (*Opening a back door for* ANDY) There you are, Andy.

ANDY: (*Coldly*) I'll sit in the front . . . and it's 'Mr Morrison' to you.

33. INT. THE MARTINS' LIVING ROOM. LATE AFTERNOON

ANDY *sitting in front of the fire.* LORNA *is peeling the potatoes.* MAUREEN *is sitting watching* ANDY. ANN *is also there.*

ANN: Do you want some more tea, Uncle Andy?

LORNA: (*Calling out*) The light's out under the pot . . . I'm putting the dinner on.

ANDY: Another cup would have been lovely.

ANN: (*Going*) Sure I can boil a wee drop for you.

ANDY: A wee fresh drop mind . . . stewed tea's bad for my chest.

MAUREEN: Are you going to die, Uncle Andy?

ANDY: Ah now . . . who's to know that, child dear?

MAUREEN: My mummy died and she wasn't nearly as old as you.

ANDY: Poor Janet . . . ach, sure I've lost both my sisters . . . your Aunty Sarah . . . or she would have been. She died long before you were born.

MAUREEN: When I used to go to the hospital Mummy called me Sarah.

ANDY: Poor Janet and poor Sarah. There's only me now. The last of the lot. (*Clatter of something falling in the kitchen.*)

LORNA: (*Impatiently to* ANN *in the scullery*) It would suit you better to help me than dance attendance on him. I've a dinner to get. Will you hurry up?

34. INT. PAULINE'S FLAT. EVENING

BILLY *in Pauline's flat.*

PAULINE: Do you want to go? (*Pause.*) Billy . . . wouldn't we be better just saying goodbye?

BILLY: Would we?

PAULINE: I think so.

BILLY: You're the nurse, you know the treatment.

PAULINE: What is wrong with you, Billy? You don't know what you want, and you're suspicious of what I want. (*Pause.*) Stay . . . I'll play some music.

BILLY: I'd better go . . . it's Andy's first night home and all.

PAULINE: Oh to hell with Andy . . . I suppose he wouldn't approve of you being with me, right enough.

BILLY: I decide who I see.

PAULINE: (*Rising*) Will I run you up?

BILLY: No, I can walk.

(*She sits.* BILLY *puts on his coat. Stops at the door.*)

Pauline . . . (*Pause.*) I'll see you again.

PAULINE: (*Close to tears*) Yes . . . I know you will, Billy.

35. EXT. STREET CORNER. EVENING

About 10 p.m. IAN *is standing there when* BILLY *appears.* BILLY*'s had a few drinks.*

IAN: What about you, Billy?

BILLY: Ian . . . where's Valerie?

IAN: Watching some oul daft thing about having babies on telly. I was near sick . . . out for a mouthful of air. (*Pause*) Not out with the girl the night?

BILLY: I saw her for a while, then went for a few pints.

IAN: Bloody woman's desperate, eh?

(FLETCHER *approaches.*)

Here's Romeo.

JOHN: Billy, Ian.

BILLY: D'you know Ian's getting married, Fletcher?

JOHN: Yes . . . congratulations, Ian.

IAN: Congratulations . . . shit, Fletcher.

(BILLY *and* IAN *laugh.*)

(*Mimics*) 'Congratulations, Ian.'

BILLY: I'll tell you something, Fletcher . . . you ever do anything like that to my sister . . . (*Grabbing* FLETCHER, *but not roughly*) I'll kill you . . . just lay a finger on her and you're dead.

IAN: Here Billy, let me take him.

(BILLY *lets go.*)

JOHN: Look, lads . . . I don't want trouble . . . no fighting.

IAN: You used to be a hard man, Fletcher.

JOHN: (*To* BILLY) I don't fight now, Billy.

BILLY: You don't fight . . . you don't drink . . . you've become a bloody saint.

IAN: Are you backing down, Fletcher? Are you scared?

JOHN: Just leave it, Ian . . . please, mate.

IAN: (*Thumping* JOHN *on the chest*) I'm not your mate.

JOHN: Now listen, son . . . don't push it.

IAN: Come on round the entry and say that.

JOHN: You've asked for it . . .

BILLY: (*As they move off*) John . . . Ian . . .

(*They stop. He approaches.*)

That's enough . . . drop it.

IAN: It's him I'm going to drop.

BILLY: (*Sharply*) You heard me.

IAN: He's called me, Billy . . . you heard him.

BILLY: Where do you think you are . . . Dodge City? Go home, John. I spoke out of turn. No hard feelings.

JOHN: 'Night, Billy.

(*He glares at* IAN *and moves off.*)

IAN: I could have taken him, Billy.

BILLY: I'll tell you something I learnt from my da . . . half a hard man's harder than no hard man at all. (*Pause.*) Fletcher'd still wreck you, son. Wreck you. (*Pause.*) I'm going for a walk.

(*He leaves* IAN *standing.*)

36. INT. THE MARTINS' LIVING ROOM. NIGHT

LORNA *enters from the scullery with a hot-water bottle.* ANDY *is smoking his pipe.*

LORNA: I'll just put this jar in your bed.

ANDY: (*Spitting into the fire, to* LORNA*'s disgust*) This is some welcome on my first night . . . him never in yet. I'll go up in a minute. Is there a chamber pot?

LORNA: A what. . . ? No, we haven't had one of those for years.

ANDY: And what am I supposed to use if I need to go during the night? You don't expect me to go out into that cold yard, do you?

LORNA: We don't have one . . . I never thought about it.

ANDY: Do you have a bucket? I'll have to have something.

37. EXT. JUNE'S HOUSE. NIGHT

The garden gate of June's house, off the Lisburn Road.

JUNE: You never wrote, what was I supposed to think?

BILLY: You could have called round when you were home.

JUNE: I ran after you before Billy . . . what good did it do me?

BILLY: I was never a letter-writer. (*Pause.*) When do you go back?

JUNE: Next Thursday. I should have been back a week ago, but Mum got a bad flu.

BILLY: Is it good then?

JUNE: It was hell at first . . . I was homesick . . . and I missed you . . . but I'm well settled now.

BILLY: Do you have a boyfriend over there?

JUNE: Yes . . . and we're doing the same course so we have a lot in common.

BILLY: He's more your type then . . . not common and ignorant like me?

JUNE: He's coming over in the New Year to meet Mum . . . then we're getting engaged.

BILLY: That should keep her happy.

(*Pause.*)

JUNE: It's cold out here.

BILLY: I've never had to stand out here before.

JUNE: I don't want Mum to have a relapse.

(*Pause. They have nothing to say.*)

I'd better go in . . . in case she wakes up.

BILLY: Right . . . I'll run on . . . be seeing you.

(*He goes. She doesn't reply, but watches him walk off.*)

38. INT. THE MARTINS' HOUSE. MORNING

Friday morning. BILLY *getting ready to leave for work.*

LORNA: I really like Pauline . . . she's a great laugh. We'd a great time yesterday. (*Pause.*) Who was your letter from?

BILLY: June . . . you know what educated people are like . . . talking's not enough for them, they have to write everything down.

LORNA: Did you really want back with her?

BILLY: I don't know . . . maybe I was just being greedy.

(*Pause.*)

LORNA: I'd rather have Pauline.

BILLY: (*Looks at her*) Aye . . . it's time I wasn't here. I hope Uncle Andy gives that Watson a good telling off.

LORNA: I'd rather go on my own . . . goodness knows what he'll come out with.

BILLY: You just look out for Ann . . . don't let them make a fool of her.

(*She leaves him to the door.*)

39. EXT. BOTANIC AVENUE. DAY

IAN *and* VALERIE *trudging up Botanic Avenue with tins of paint and rolls of wallpaper.*

VALERIE: There's no point starting a job like this in the middle of the day.

IAN: Maybe Billy'll give me a hand with it.

VALERIE: I'm damned sure he'll not. That's one oul game that's not going to start . . . people running all the time. You'll do it yourself.

IAN: What, the whole lot?

VALERIE: Why, did you think you'd leave it half done?

IAN: I've never papered before.

VALERIE: My da told you how to do it. (*Pause.*) I'll maybe get Lorna to sew up the curtains . . . she's a great sewer.

IAN: Aye, you're going to get help with your bit.

VALERIE: Oh shut up gerning.

40. INT. MR WATSON'S OFFICE. DAY

A knock.

CYRIL: Come in.

(LORNA, ANN, *and* ANDY *enter.*)

Sit down. (*To* ANDY) Are you Mr Martin?

ANDY: Not at all, I'm Mr Morrison, their Uncle Andy. I live with them at present, keep an eye on them . . . keep them in order.

CYRIL: Quite, well I'm sure this young lady has told you all that happened. She used abusive language to Miss Semple. She also threw a book, striking Miss Semple on the shoulder, and to make matters worse the book she threw was the Bible. Such conduct will not be tolerated. I was actually off on Friday afternoon when it happened, otherwise she'd have had a pair of sore hands to go with her suspension. (*Pause.*) Now . . . before I'm prepared to readmit her . . .

ANDY: Did you know your Miss Semple insulted the child's father?

CYRIL: I wouldn't have considered what Miss Semple said to have been offensive.

ANDY: She didn't say it about your da.

CYRIL: Mr Morrison, please let me get on and conclude this matter . . . now, readmission depends on the assurances of all three of you that it will never happen again. Also of course I'll expect this young lady to make a full and acceptable apology to Miss Semple.

LORNA: Of course, Mr Watson, she's sorry and it will never happen again.

CYRIL: Well, young lady . . . and what have you to say for yourself?

ANN: (*Mumbling*) I'm sorry.

CYRIL: Speak up . . . you had no difficulty making yourself heard last Friday.

LORNA: She says she's sorry.

CYRIL: She can speak for herself. (*Rising*) Right . . . I'll have Miss Semple round and we can all bear witness to this apology.

(ANN *cries a little.*)

ANDY: In the name of Jasus . . .

LORNA: Uncle Andy . . . for goodness' sake . . .

ANDY: Away out of that, he's heard language before. What is it you want from the child? Do you think we should call a United Nations peace-keeping force to stand between her and this Semple woman?

CYRIL: Mr Morrison, you're not making matters any better for her.

ANDY: Is the child not to be allowed to defend her own da? Should it not be your Miss Semple apologizing to her for provoking her?

LORNA: Uncle Andy . . . look, Mr Watson, Ann has said she's sorry and you can see she means it . . . she doesn't have to say it again. Now I'd like her back at school again immediately.

ANDY: Maybe we should take her down to your bosses in Academy Street and see if they can't place her in a school where her da's good name won't be dragged through the mud. I'm telling you your Miss Semple's the lucky woman he's not here himself.

LORNA: Mr Watson, will you please let Ann back to school?

CYRIL: (*Glancing at each*) All right . . . I'll pass on Ann's apology to Miss Semple and . . . and we'll say no more about it. She can return to school on Monday morning.

LORNA: Thank you, Mr Watson.

ANDY: Mind you, yous teachers aren't what yous used to be . . . in my day teachers were liked and respected.

LORNA: Uncle Andy, we're going.

ANDY: Eh! Oh aye . . . well . . . good day to you.

41. INT. THE FLAT. DAY

IAN *and* VALERIE *in the flat. Some of it is decorated. He's painting a window frame cream.* VALERIE *is sitting smoking, watching him.*

IAN: You know, they say you shouldn't smoke when you're pregnant.

(*Pause. She ignores him.*)

They say it's bad for the baby.

(*Pause. She regards him.*)

VALERIE: (*Sucking hard on her cigarette and blowing the smoke in his direction*) They also say you shouldn't get pregnant before you're married. (*Pause.*) If you could paint with your tongue you'd be finished by now. Get on with it. (*Pause.*) I don't like that colour. I think we'll try something else.

IAN: What? I haven't even the bloody thing finished and you're changing your mind?

VALERIE: It's all right for you . . . you're going to be out at work all day . . . I'm the one has to look at it.

IAN: But sure you picked it to go with the paper?

VALERIE: I know . . . we might have to change that and all.

IAN: (*Disgusted*) Ah for . . .

42. EXT. THE LISBURN ROAD END OF COLLEGE GARDENS. DAY

BILLY *and* JUNE *together.* BILLY *still in his working clothes.*

JUNE: I must be mad, absolutely insane.

BILLY: Do you want to go for a drink?

JUNE: No, let's just stroll around the block. I'm going away tonight . . . my mum's leaving me to the boat.

BILLY: What about the English boyfriend?

JUNE: I don't know right now. (*Strolling down College Gardens*) Will you write to me this time, Billy?

BILLY: I'm not a great letter-writer.

JUNE: I don't want literature . . . just contact.

BILLY: All right . . .

(BILLY *and* JUNE *come face to face with* PAULINE.)

Hello.

PAULINE: Hello, Billy.

(*Pause.*)

BILLY: Ah . . . this is June . . . June, this is Pauline.

(*They greet each other—just.*)

Pauline's a nurse . . . she looked after Uncle Andy.

PAULINE: (*Hurt*) You should collect butterflies, Billy.

(*She sweeps past them. They stand.*)

JUNE: Now that Lorna's found a boyfriend it's nice to see you've found someone else to nurse you.

BILLY: You cheeky bitch . . . don't you think your fancy university education gives you the right to talk down to me.

JUNE: Oh, I'll never beat you, Billy, even with my education . . . but I'm damned if I'll stop trying to defend myself.

(*Sound of a car trying to start.*)

I think your 'nurse' needs a push.

BILLY: Go back to your pansy English boyfriend . . . somebody your snobbish oul ma is stupid enough to appreciate.

(JUNE *turns and goes back the way they came. He grabs hold of the railings of Methody. He walks towards* PAULINE, *still trying to start her car.*)

(*Through the window*) Do you want a push?

PAULINE: Push off, Billy.

(*She clambers out and locks the car.*)

BILLY: Pauline . . . she's just an old friend.

PAULINE: And I'm just your Uncle Andy's old nurse.

(*She walks off and leaves him.*)

43. INT. A BAR. EVENING

ANDY: Emphysema and complications they called it. Now you're as wise as I am. It sounds like a bad bet in the Grand National.

BILLY: Didn't you ask them?

ANDY: As far as I'm concerned it's a fancy word they've used to get me back in . . . but I'm not going.

BILLY: Uncle Andy . . .

ANDY: Look, son . . . I didn't come here to talk about the mumbo-jumbo of bloody witch-doctors . . . it's taking the flavour of my drink.

IAN: (*Approaching*) What about you Billy . . . Andy?

ANDY: Jasus, it's the silver chamois.

BILLY: Are you having one?

IAN: Naw . . . I'm away up to see the oul doll . . . (*Showing chamois*) Doing the windies. I finish here the day. Did you not see the ladders outside?

ANDY: Oh aye . . . we saw a fella walkin' off with a pair of ladders as we were coming in.

IAN: Walking off . . . Christ the night.

(IAN *rushes out.*)

ANDY: (*Laughing*) Would you look at that . . . and to think the likes of that's bringing childer intil the world. (*Pause.*) What about you and your nurse?

BILLY: You'll be pleased to hear we fell out, about a fortnight ago.

ANDY: She still calls up . . . to see Lorna. You know, I reckon you could do worse.

BILLY: Aye, well I'll hang on until I can do better. (*Drinking*) Another one?

ANDY: Naw . . . it's got no taste tonight . . . I'm going home till my bed.

(*They move to the door.*)

BILLY: Look . . . I'm just going to go a wee message . . . can you get back all right?

ANDY: Aye . . . aye. (*A hand on* BILLY*'s arm*) Listen, I know the score . . . I've put my house in the hands of an agent. All I have and whatever the house gets is for you and Lorna.

44. INT. THE MARTINS' LIVING ROOM. EVENING

JOHN *and* LORNA *sitting. He produces a box from his pocket.*

JOHN: Here . . . ah . . . this is for you . . . a wee surprise like.

(LORNA *opens it and finds an engagement ring.*)

LORNA: An engagement ring.

JOHN: If it doesn't fit we can get it changed.

(*Pause.*)

LORNA: John . . . I can't take this.

JOHN: What? Why not? I mean we don't have to decide anything else, not yet.

LORNA: (*Upset*) Why did you do that . . . why didn't you ask me?

JOHN: I wanted it to be a surprise.

LORNA: John . . . John . . . look, I like you . . . I enjoy going out in the car and all that . . . (*Hopeless.*)

JOHN: I'm all right for drives in the car, but not good enough to marry?

LORNA: Marry . . . we've never even mentioned marriage . . . I've never even thought about marrying you.

JOHN: It's him, isn't it? Big brother bloody Billy. He doesn't think I'm good enough for you. I'm as good as bloody him.

LORNA: It's nothing to do with Billy . . . it's me. I don't love you, John . . . it's never been like that. I'm sorry.

(*He stands, shattered—almost tearful.*)

JOHN: You've made a fool of me . . . a bloody stupid fool.

LORNA: No . . .

JOHN: (*Screaming*) Yes you bloody have . . . you're just another bloody Martin.

ANN: (*On the stairs*) Lorna, why's he shouting . . . are you all right?

LORNA: Yes, I'm fine, go back to bed, love . . . I'm fine.

(*She offers the box.* JOHN *glares up at* ANN, *tears in his eyes, then stumbles blindly out into the night. Long pause.*)

ANN: He was crying, Lorna.

(LORNA *seems close to tears herself.* ANN *comes downstairs.*)

Don't you cry, Lorna.

(*They embrace.* ANDY *enters, surveys the scene.*)

ANDY: In the name of Jasus . . . I'll make a cup of tea.

45. INT. PAULINE'S FLAT. EVENING

BILLY: I watched my ma dying, I don't want to go through that again. I've got to like him . . . to like having him around.

PAULINE: Is that all you came round for . . . to consult me?

BILLY: Do you want me to stay away?

PAULINE: I know I'm a fool, Billy, but don't rub my nose in it.

BILLY: I'm sorry, Pauline, I mean that.

PAULINE: What is it you mean, Billy? I'm never totally certain with you. You're like a pet dog that gets so excited it bites, instead of licking. It wouldn't be so bad of you were a small, gentle dog . . . (*Pause.*) I got a letter today . . . I've been offered the Canadian job. I start at the beginning of February.

BILLY: Have you accepted?

PAULINE: They assume that . . . unless I let them know otherwise.

BILLY: I'd better go. (*Pause.*) I hope it works out.

PAULINE: I'll make sure it does, Billy . . . (*As* BILLY *goes*) And I'll find a boyfriend who makes me smile and lets me laugh.

46. EXT. THE STREET. NIGHT

IAN, *coming down, whistling. Just as he reaches the entry,* JOHN *steps out.*

JOHN: You . . . couldn't be better.

IAN: (*Nervous*) John . . . what about you?

JOHN: It's third time lucky for you . . . you've wanted a go twice . . . now's your chance.

IAN: I'm in a wee bit of a hurry John . . . the wife's not too well. (*Without warning* FLETCHER *lashes out.* IAN *staggers against the wall.* JOHN *throws him into the entry, goes after him and hammers him.* IAN*'s moaning and crying can be heard, and then cease.* JOHN *emerges, straightens himself and strolls away.*)

47. INT. THE MARTINS' LIVING ROOM. NIGHT

Late that night. LORNA *sitting,* BILLY *enters.*

LORNA: How is he?

BILLY: He'll be all right. They're keeping him in overnight. Valerie's up to stay with her ma.

LORNA: You're not to get involved now . . . it's none of your business.

BILLY: I'm not bothering. Ian's been wanting a go at John for a while now . . . I warned him. I hopes he's learnt his lesson.

LORNA: I'd a long talk with Uncle Andy tonight. He'll have to go back into the hospital.

BILLY: He's frightened . . . I think he feels he'll die in there this time.

LORNA: He was very upset . . . I've promised him if he goes in for a couple of weeks I'll bring him back out here and look after him.

BILLY: What'd he say?

LORNA: He's agreed . . . I even got a goodnight kiss tonight.

BILLY: Huh, Fletcher's not right out the door and you're at somebody else.

LORNA: I don't want that mentioned. (*Pause.*) What about you?

BILLY: I'm going to bed.

LORNA: Are you going to let Pauline go to Canada?

BILLY: Why not, it's what she wants to do.

LORNA: For goodness' sake Billy . . . it's a matter of choice for you.

BILLY: Just because you and her are mates now . . .

LORNA: It's not just that . . . she loves you and you love her . . . it's not going to make you any less of a man to admit that. You're so like Dad . . . but even he seems to have learnt sense at last. I can manage here. It's not as if you're going to be a million miles away. We have to break sometime, Billy.

48. INT. THE MARTINS' LIVING ROOM. DAY

ANDY *is sitting puffing on his pipe. The door opens and* ANN *enters, followed by* MAUREEN.

ANDY: Will you quit that endless running in and out. (*Turns and sees* ANN.) Oh, it's you.

ANN: I live here too.

ANDY: I thought it was that other one.

MAUREEN: I'm away out.

(*She goes.*)

ANDY: See what I mean . . . in and out, in and out. Like a bloody jack-in-the-box.

ANN: Give over gerning. Do you want a cup of tea?

ANDY: Tea . . . aye, I'll take one to keep you happy.

(*As she goes into the scullery he coughs and spits into the fire.*)

ANN: Will you cut that out . . . it's disgusting.

ANDY: I have to get rid of it.

ANN: You can do it without being so disgusting.

ANDY: Huh, and you're the one wants to be a nurse.

49. INT. THE MARTINS' LIVING ROOM. EVENING

ANN *is sitting at the table, books spread out, sucking her pencil.* BILLY *reading the paper.* LORNA *in the scullery.*

BILLY: Have you never finished that homework yet?

ANN: I can't think of anything to write.

BILLY: What have you to do?

ANN: An essay, 'I am a postage stamp'.

BILLY: Who give you that?

ANN: Miss Simple Semple . . . stupid oul bat.

BILLY: Isn't she the one you'd the trouble over? Are you getting on with her all right now?

ANN: Aye, but I won't be if I don't write something quick.

BILLY: It's easy.

ANN: Right, what would you write?

BILLY: (*Thinking*) 'I am a postage stamp. I've just been licked, stuck, and sent.'

ANN: Brilliant . . . can you write that on an elastic band so that I can make it stretch over two pages?

(LORNA *comes through carrying some clothes. These she leaves on a chair.*)

Lorna, what would you do if you were a postage stamp?

LORNA: Get somebody to send me to the Bahamas.

ANN: That's it . . . Lorna, you're brilliant.

LORNA: What's she going on about?

BILLY: Just a silly essay she's got.
(*A car draws up. Horn toots,* BILLY *rises.*)
There she is . . . I'm away . . . I'll not be late.
(*He goes.*)

50. INT. THE MARTINS' LIVING ROOM. EVENING

ANN, MAUREEN *and* JOAN *there. The two older ones are trying on nail varnish.*

MAUREEN: Let me try it, Ann?

ANN: No, Lorna doesn't allow you to have it.

JOAN: Valerie and Ian had to get married 'cause she's pregnant. My ma told me. That's why it wasn't a white wedding.

MAUREEN: Why not?

JOAN: White's pure. If you're pregnant you're not pure.

MAUREEN: Our Lorna says she's not getting married in white.

ANN: You shouldn't be listening to us, you're too young.

JOAN: (*Lighting a butt*) Away you out and keep watch, Maureen . . . go on.
(MAUREEN *goes.*)
I'll have a quick puff before anybody comes in. Are you going to have a drag?
(ANN *takes it.*)

MAUREEN: (*Rushing in*) Here's our Billy.
(ANN *nearly chokes. She throws the butt into the fire. They sit.* BILLY *enters.*)

BILLY: Who's been smoking?

ANN: Smoking? It must have been Uncle Andy.

BILLY: I'm damned sure it wasn't. He only takes the pipe now. I hope it wasn't you, girl?

ANN: Me . . . it was not . . .

JOAN: (*Quickly*) It was me, Billy, I was just having a wee pull.

BILLY: Well just get yourself to hell out of this. This is no hideout for smokers. (*To* MAUREEN:) Have you your homework done?

MAUREEN: I've just tables to do.

BILLY: (*As* JOAN *goes*) Get them done. (*To* ANN) What about you?

ANN: I've just some sums.

BILLY: I catch you smoking, you've had it.

51. INT. PAULINE'S FLAT. EVENING

PAULINE *writing.* BILLY *peeping out behind the curtains.*

PAULINE: (*Sitting up*) Finished.

BILLY: What did you say?

PAULINE: 'Dear sir, thank you for your kind offer of a job . . . but I prefer to live in sin, rather than Toronto.'
(*They laugh.*)
Come away from that window.

BILLY: Do you think they'll be all right?

PAULINE: Of course they will . . . and looking out there doesn't help.

BILLY: How long do you reckon Uncle Andy'll be in?

PAULINE: Will you stop it . . . that's four times you've asked me that. They live a mile or so away . . . you'll see them every day.

BILLY: I suppose Andy's sitting spitting, putting out the last of the fire.

PAULINE: If you keep this up I'm going to chase you. (*Pause.*) Should we look for a bigger flat?

BILLY: (*Rising and coming to her*) Not tonight.
(*They embrace.*)

PAULINE: Fool . . . do you think your dad will like me?

BILLY: I hope not . . . we've never agreed about anything.

PAULINE: I love you, Billy.

BILLY: Nought out of ten for intelligence. It's a pity Andy isn't going to your hospital. He might have been on your ward again.

PAULINE: I think I'll survive without that.

BILLY: He'll say you're a scheming wee Fenian who seduced his nephew. What'll you say to that?

PAULINE: It was your own choice.

BILLY: I'm going to bed.

PAULINE: Taking anybody with you?

BILLY: Just my nurse . . . in case I take bad during the night.

PAULINE: They say every home should have one. I'll just fetch a glass for my false teeth. (*Starts to giggle.*) Oh... you should see your face. (*Gnashing her teeth*) Relax, they're all my own.

52. INT. THE MARTINS' LIVING ROOM. NIGHT

ANDY *smoking his pipe. Clink of bottles being set on the sill.* LORNA *comes in, locking up behind her.*

ANDY: At least we can get the place locked up early when he's not here. I hope he knows what he's doing.

LORNA: Of course he does.

ANDY: You young ones nowadays . . . you wouldn't have done it in my day. Your da'll not approve, I don't care what you say.

LORNA: Have you all ready for tomorrow?

ANDY: Don't remind me. You promise it's only for the two weeks?

LORNA: Two or three.

ANDY: Jasus, it's up to three already.

LORNA: It's up to the doctor, I can't say.

ANDY: I'll miss this wee house. It's a quare cosy wee place. Are you sure you'll be able to manage all on your own?

LORNA: Of course I will. (*Pause*) Are you ready for bed? It seems a shame to leave a nice fire like that.

ANDY: Do you know, love . . . do you know what I'd really fancy?

LORNA: What?

ANDY: A nice quiet wee game of draughts . . . can you play draughts?

LORNA: Yes. (*Fetching the board*) Black or white?

ANDY: Oh, I'll be white. (*Stuff being set out.*) You know I was the champion of this game the last time I was in hospital.

LORNA: Black goes first.

ANDY: Fire away.

(*She goes.*)

I saw that photo in your da's letter . . . thon's a fine-looking woman.

LORNA: Yes . . . it's your move.

ANDY: Aye, I know . . . I'm studying the board . . . you can't rush in this game, that's the whole secret . . . study the board . . . make the right choice. (*Pause.*) I'member playing a game of this in the Far East . . . a week it lasted . . . a full week . . . it doesn't do to rush things.

LORNA: The fire's not going to last a week . . . and you've a hospital to go to in the morning.

(*She moves. He takes one of hers and chuckles. Puffs contentedly at his pipe and sits back to contemplate the board.*)

53. INT. PAULINE'S FLAT. NIGHT

Some hours later, BILLY *and* PAULINE *in bed. Darkness.*

PAULINE: Are you asleep, Billy?

BILLY: Yes.

PAULINE: Then why are you talking?

BILLY: I talk in my sleep.

PAULINE: It's cold and wet outside. I'm so warm and contented.

BILLY: Better than Toronto?

PAULINE: Much. Are you happy, Billy?

(*Pause.*)

BILLY: Yea . . . please, nurse, can I have a sleep now?

(*Giggles. Quiet.*)

A COMING TO TERMS FOR BILLY

Characters

NORMAN
MAVIS
BILLY
LORNA
ANN
MAUREEN
UNCLE ANDY
PAULINE
JOHN FLETCHER
JOAN
IAN
BIG DAVIE
TOMMY AGNEW

A Coming to Terms for Billy was first shown on BBC Television early in 1984. The cast was as follows:

NORMAN	James Ellis
MAVIS	Gwen Taylor
BILLY	Kenneth Branagh
LORNA	Brid Brennan
ANN	Tracey Lynch
MAUREEN	Aine Gorman
UNCLE ANDY	Mark Mulholland
PAULINE	Julia Dearden
JOHN FLETCHER	John Hewitt
JOAN	Deirdre Morgan
IAN	Colum Convey
BIG DAVIE	Derek Lord
TOMMY AGNEW	George Shane
Producer	Chris Parr
Director	Paul Seed
Designer	Mike Selina

1. EXT. BOAT. MORNING

The deck of the Liverpool Boat, entering Belfast Lough. NORMAN *is leaning on the rail. He smokes, gazing thoughtfully ashore at the Irish coast—County Down side. Hold a moment.* MAVIS *appears through the hatch and joins him. For a moment she says nothing, just gazing with him. She is a good-looking woman, in her early forties, English.*

MAVIS: Are you all right?

NORMAN: Aye, I'm fine . . . fine. Did I waken you getting up?

MAVIS: No, no . . . I was awake. I thought maybe you felt sick . . . seasick.

NORMAN: No.

MAVIS: Frightened?

NORMAN: Frightened . . . me?

MAVIS: Well . . . apprehensive?

NORMAN: No . . . just wondering.

MAVIS: I'm frightened . . . I've never been so frightened in my life before.

NORMAN: Ah, come on . . . I've told you, there's nothing to be frightened about . . . they'll love you.

(*She's obviously unconvinced.*)

It'll be the same for them. They'll be nervous. You'll all be friends in no time at all. (*Pause.*) For goodness' sake, love . . . we're big grown-up people. You're going to be their mother, not their big sister. You're not supposed to be terrified of them. Jasus, they're only youngsters after all.

MAVIS: I can't just force myself on the . . . I have to *win* their friendship. That's what frightens me . . . not them as such.

NORMAN: In the end they'll do what they're told.

MAVIS: No, love, I don't want it to be like that. You can't force people to love you . . . to display feelings they don't really have.

NORMAN: (*Breaking the mood, throwing an arm around her*) Come on . . . a dirty great big Irish breakfast . . . that's what you need. Soda bread, tattie bread, egg, sausage, bacon . . . smothered in that much sauce it makes your eyes water.

MAVIS: It sounds revolting.

(*He leads her towards the hatch, laughing, arms around each other.*)

2. INT. BILLY'S AND PAULINE'S FLAT. MORNING

The flat is a large one. BILLY *is in his working clothes.*

BILLY: Should I grow a beard?

PAULINE: Billy . . . you do realize that your dad and . . . his woman are arriving here today?

BILLY: Why do you think I'm wearing black boots?

PAULINE: You haven't mentioned the fact, that's all.

BILLY: I keep thinking you'll shake me and I'll realize it was a dream.

PAULINE: For goodness' sake . . . we'd better apologize for that double bed . . . it's . . . well, it's suggestive.

BILLY: I know . . . you can sleep with Save-us Mavis . . . and I'll kip with Daddy . . . or you can . . .

PAULINE: (*Laughing*) Shut up, you fool.

BILLY: Do you know how many years it is since me and my daddy curled toes under the same sheets?

PAULINE: I'm going to like your dad . . . just to spite you.

BILLY: And maybe I'll fall for Save-us.

(*She swipes at him and they embrace.*)

PAULINE: Straight home. . . .

3. INT. THE MARTINS' LIVING ROOM. MORNING

LORNA, ANN *and* MAUREEN *at breakfast.*

LORNA: It's a pity you two couldn't rise as well as this when you're at school.

ANN: I want to see what she's like before she's my ma.

MAUREEN: Do you think if we don't like her my da'll not marry her?

LORNA: I'm sure Dad'll please himself.

ANN: I think Billy should be going down to meet them.

LORNA: He's his work to go to.

ANN: It doesn't matter . . . he could take a day off. I'll bet you my da would have done it for him.

LORNA: If Pauline hadn't been around, Billy'd probably have went down.

ANN: My da doesn't know Pauline.

LORNA: Sure I'll be with her.

MAUREEN: And she's got a car. I'd rather see her and get a lift than see Billy and have to walk.

(*There is a thud above. They all look up.*)

ANN: Uncle Andy's fell out of bed.

LORNA: What on earth's he getting up at this time for?

MAUREEN: Maybe he can't wait to see my da.

LORNA: I'm sure.

ANN: I wish I was going to the boat.

LORNA: You can give this place a good tidying when we're out.

ANN: Thanks a lot . . that was worth getting up for.

(ANDY *comes down.*)

LORNA: Uncle Andy, what are you doing up so early?

ANDY: Ah, I couldn't sleep. I tossed and turned most of the night.

MAUREEN: Are you all excited about seeing my da and Mavis?

ANDY: (*Looking at* LORNA) I can barely wait. (*Pause.*) Any chance of a cup of tea?

LORNA: Ann'll get you it.

ANN: Aye, just call rent-a-slave.

ANDY: Give's a slice of toast and my All-Bran.

ANN: For goodness' sake.

ANDY: Mind and boil the milk . . . and sprinkle the sugar on, don't just dump it in the middle. (*Pause.*) Are you lighting that fire afore you go out, girl?

LORNA: Yes . . . Maureen, hurry up and finish that and then rake the fire out.

MAUREEN: It's too warm for a fire . . . I'm roasting.

ANDY: You might be . . . I'm foundered.

ANN: Do you want marmalade on your toast?

ANDY: Is it orange marmalade?

ANN: No, it's green, made in Dublin.

LORNA: Ann . . .

ANDY: Cheeky skitter . . .

(MAUREEN *rakes the fire vigorously, creating clouds of dust.*)

In the name of Jasus . . .

LORNA: Maureen, go easy, you're making too much dust.

4. INT. THE MARTINS' LIVING ROOM. DAY

PAULINE *and* LORNA *are ready to leave to go and pick Norman and Mavis up.* ANDY *is sitting by the fire.* MAUREEN *and* ANN *are clearing up.*

LORNA: Right, we're away. Ann, boil a kettle and we can have a cup of tea as soon as we get in. Dad always loved tea.

MAUREEN: Does Mavis take sugar?

LORNA: How do I know that?

ANN: (*Nodding towards* ANDY) And tell him not to be spitting in front of her.

ANDY: Never mind her . . . fancy English woman, huh. If my lungs clog up and I have to spit, I'll spit.

PAULINE: I must bring you a few sputum mugs . . . then you can do it quietly if you have to.

ANDY: Oh . . . hide away my bad health . . .

LORNA: Come on, Pauline, he's just awkward.

(LORNA *and* PAULINE *go.*)

ANN: (*Watching from the window*) I'm going to get a car as soon as I'm old enough.

MAUREEN: I'm not. I'm going to get a boyfriend with one.

ANDY: Listen to it . . . hardly out of nappies and wanting to take advantage of some poor fella. Then this one coming today . . . I wonder how she got her claws into your da . . . (*Rising and making for the stairs*) I suppose he was too drunk to know what he was doing . . . until it was too late.

5. INT. THE BOAT TERMINAL. DAY

NORMAN *and* LORNA *are clinging to each other.* MAVIS *and* PAULINE *are standing, smiling shyly at each other.*

NORMAN: (*Kissing* LORNA) It's great to see you, girl. (*Holding her at arm's length*) You're looking great.

LORNA: (*Emotional*) So are you, Dad . . . you've put on weight.

NORMAN: That's all the good food Mavis . . . (*Realizing*) Oh . . . I'm sorry . . . getting carried away. Mavis . . . Lorna . . . Lorna . . . Mavis.

LORNA: I'm pleased to meet you . . . welcome to Belfast.

MAVIS: Thank you, Lorna. I've heard so much about you, I feel I know you quite well already.

LORNA: Dad . . . Mavis . . . this is Pauline . . . our Billy's girl.

MAVIS: Yes . . . we've said hello.

NORMAN: (*Taking her hand*) So you're the one that's after my wee fella. He's getting more like me now . . . beginning to get a bit of taste.

PAULINE: Thank you . . . I'm really pleased to meet you. (*Stuck*) I've heard a lot about you . . .

(*Awkward pause.*)

NORMAN: Well . . . Billy had to work I take it?

PAULINE: Yes . . . I'm off today you see.

LORNA: With Pauline having the car and all . . .

NORMAN: Oh, he's right . . . you have to look after the work. (*Pause. Picking up cases*) Right . . . will we go?

(PAULINE *picks out her keys and leads off with* NORMAN. LORNA *and* MAVIS *follow, chatting.*)

6. INT. THE MARTINS' LIVING ROOM. DAY

ANDY *gets to his feet as* LORNA *and* MAVIS *enter.* PAULINE *follows.* ANDY *is dressed in his best clothes, tie, etc.* LORNA *is taken aback by this display.*

LORNA: Uncle Andy . . . this is Mavis . . . Mavis, Uncle Andy.

ANDY: Come in, come in and welcome. Here, let me take that coat.

MAVIS: (*Giving it*) Thank you. I'm very pleased to meet you.

ANDY: Sit down there . . . sit down.

PAULINE: They're mobbing your dad out there.

LORNA: (*Going back to the door*) They're desperate, them two. (*Calling*) Ann . . . Maureen . . . let Dad in for goodness' sake.

(*They enter, the girls clinging to* NORMAN.)

ANDY: (*Offering his hand; this and his dress take* NORMAN *aback*) Norman . . .

NORMAN: (*Shaking hands*) Andy . . . mind you, you're a brave-looking invalid.

LORNA: I'm going to do the tea.

PAULINE: I'll give you a hand.

(NORMAN*'s eye is caught by his wedding photograph on the fireplace.* LORNA *hesitates. She pushes/guides* ANN *towards the kitchen to* PAULINE.)

LORNA: Give Pauline a hand. (*Watching* NORMAN) Billy put it there.

NORMAN: Oh aye . . .

(MAVIS *rises to look at it.*)

There's been a lot of water under the bridge since that was took.

ANDY: (*To* MAVIS) My sister Janet.

MAVIS: She was nice.

ANDY: It was a great blow.

MAVIS: Yes, I'm sure it was.

NORMAN: Sit down, love.

(*Sitting too,* MAUREEN *clinging to him.*)

It's warm with that fire.

LORNA: Uncle Andy needed it . . . (*Pause.*) He feels the cold.

(NORMAN *is not pleased at* LORNA*'s degree of affection.*)

ANDY: You can never be sure when you light the fire what the day's going to do.

(ANN*'s attitude to* MAVIS *should show an edge of resentment from the outset. And a definite feeling that acceptance is not going to be automatic.*)

ANN: (*Stress on the name as distinct from a title*) Mavis . . . do you take sugar?

MAVIS: Just one, please.

MAUREEN: That's the answer to the next question.

MAVIS: Pardon?

MAUREEN: She asked if you take sugar, you should have said 'yes', or 'no', then she'd ask you how many.

NORMAN: I want no cheek from you, young madam.

MAUREEN: No, my teacher always tells us to answer the question asked.

MAVIS: Yes, you're quite right . . . and so is your teacher.

(ANN *and* PAULINE *bring in the tea and sandwiches.*)

LORNA: Move now, Maureen, and give Dad a chance to get his tea.

(ANDY *is handed his usual mug and mutters something.*)

ANN: What? Sure you never take a cup and saucer . . . you always say saucers are for snobs.

ANDY: (*Grins foolishly at* MAVIS) Did you have a good crossing?

MAVIS: Yes, it was very nice. Well, I assume it was, we slept. It certainly seemed perfectly calm this morning.

ANDY: It can be a quare rough stretch of water. Most people fly now.

(MAUREEN *starts to laugh, followed by* ANN.)

What's so funny?

MAUREEN: You said most people fly . . . but it's birds and aeroplanes that fly, not the people.

ANDY: Very funny . . . ha, ha.

MAUREEN: My teacher says language is a tool and should be properly used.

ANDY: Teachers . . . they think they know everything and they know nothing.

ANN: Mavis . . . you're a teacher, aren't you?

MAVIS: Yes . . . well, I was . . . I did teach. I haven't for a while, but I'm going back to it.

ANN: (*Smirking at* ANDY) More tea, Mavis?

MAVIS: I'm fine for the moment, thank you.

NORMAN: I'll have a drop more, love.

ANDY: That's lovely cheese . . . did you get that from the corner shop?

ANN: No, we stole it from a mousetrap.

ANDY: House full of comedians here today. (*Pause. To* MAVIS.) So . . . you're going to get married?

(*Pause, as* MAVIS *looks at* NORMAN. *She looks confused.*)

NORMAN: No . . . we are married . . . we got married last week.

(*Everyone is surprised, general exchange of glances.* ANN *looks devastated and makes for the scullery. They all lapse into silence.*)

7. EXT. CITY HALL GROUNDS. DAY

BILLY *is sitting on a bench, lost in thought. He is still in his working clothes. He hasn't been home yet. He looks across at the clock outside H. Samuels. It shows six thirty. He opens his lunchbox and starts eating some leftover sandwiches.*

8. INT. BILLY'S AND PAULINE'S FLAT. EVENING

The table is set for dinner. PAULINE, MAVIS *and* NORMAN *sit, quiet, nervous.* PAULINE *anxious.*

PAULINE: If we wait much longer it'll be ruined. I don't know what's happened to him.

NORMAN: It's maybe a bit of overtime . . . something that came up at the last minute. These things happen.

PAULINE: He hasn't done overtime for months.

NORMAN: But it's maybe just a last-minute thing.

MAVIS: Maybe he met a friend and went for a drink. It's . . . possible . . . he's even forgotten.

PAULINE: (*Meeting* MAVIS*'s sympathetic look. Rising*) Well, there's no point letting four dinners be ruined.

MAVIS: (*Rising*) I'll give you a hand.

NORMAN: Look . . . (*Rises.*) I wouldn't worry about it, love. I'm sure he's all right.

PAULINE: Yes . . . I'm sure he's all right, I'm not worried . . . just angry.

(*Out on* NORMAN*'s concerned expression.*)

9. EXT. STREET CORNER. EVENING

ANN, MAUREEN *and* JOAN.

JOAN: Well, what's she like?

ANN: An oul bat.

MAUREEN: She is not . . . I like her.

JOAN: You're lucky, I wish I could trade my ma in and get a new one. When are they getting married?

ANN: (*Sullen, reluctant*) They're married already.

MAUREEN: They got married in England. She's our ma now.

JOAN: (*Goading*) What about the big wedding . . . and yous as bridesmaids and all? (*Laughs.*)

ANN: Why don't you shut your trap.

JOAN: All right . . . I'm only joking.

ANN: It's not bloody funny. I'll not call her 'mammy' anyway.

MAUREEN: You'll have to, my da'll make you.

ANN: Aye, will he . . . that's what you think.

MAUREEN: Our Lorna's mad at you already.

ANN: Even Uncle Andy got all dressed up, like an oul edjit . . . just because she's English.

JOAN: What's that got to do with it?

ANN: I don't know. They all think it's something special. I don't want any Englishwoman telling me what to do.

JOAN: She'll not be here long sure. Once they go back to England you can do what you like.

ANN: Our Billy'll not call her ma either . . . that's for sure.

MAUREEN: 'Save-us Mavis' he calls her.

(*They laugh.*)

JOAN: They'll probably have other kids of their own anyway.

ANN: Who?

JOAN: Your da and Mavis.

MAUREEN: How can they?

JOAN: The same way your ma and da had you, how do you think?

(ANN *and* MAUREEN *just look at each other, dumbfounded.*)

10. INT. THE MARTINS' LIVING ROOM. EVENING

LORNA *is there on her own.* BILLY *enters, still in his working clothes.*

LORNA: Billy, I didn't expect to see you tonight. Is Pauline with you?

BILLY: No . . . I'm on my own.

LORNA: Well, what do you think of Mavis?

(*He shrugs in a non-committal way.*)

She's nice, isn't she?

BILLY: (*Sheepish*) I don't know . . . I haven't seen her yet.

(*Pause.*)

LORNA: (*Searching his face*) What? Why?

BILLY: I haven't been home yet.

LORNA: But they're expecting you . . . Pauline's cooking

something special.

(*He shrugs again.*)

For goodness' sake, Billy. Why? Why?

BILLY: I don't know . . . I can't . . .

LORNA: But they're staying with you . . . (*Angry*) She's your mother for goodness' sake.

(*He's stunned.*)

They're married . . . they got married last week.

BILLY: I thought they wanted us to meet her before they got married? (*Angry*) Why didn't he tell us?

LORNA: Does it matter now? (*Pause.*) Billy, look at the time . . . you've got to go home.

(*Pause.*)

BILLY: Has he changed? Is anything going to be different?

LORNA: But everything's different . . . he's married again . . . he's nearly stopped drinking . . . it's all different. We're all different.

BILLY: That's it you see, I don't think we are. I don't think anything's changed.

LORNA: What about Pauline? How do you think she feels? I mean they're both complete strangers to her . . . and she's doing this for us. (*Pause.*) Billy . . . she's a nice woman. She likes us, and she wants us to like her.

BILLY: She knows nothing about us. She doesn't know what went on here.

LORNA: It's over . . . all that . . . Mum's dead, all that's in the past.

BILLY: Not for me it's not . . .

(ANDY *bounces in.* JOHN FLETCHER *is with him. They stop. Silence.*)

ANDY: Is this a private row, or can anybody join in?

FLETCHER: Billy. Lorna. Right night, eh?

BILLY: What the hell's he doing in here?

ANDY: Ah now just a minute, son . . . easy on.

LORNA: Uncle Andy, away out and take John with you.

ANDY: Out . . . we're just in . . . out where?

LORNA: We're talking . . .

ANDY: Aye, well, talk away . . .

LORNA: (*Angry*) Will you get out of here . . . please?

(ANDY *is stunned. Pause.*)

Away and have a pint.

(JOHN *slips out quietly, leaving the door open for* ANDY, *waiting on the footpath.*)

ANDY: Listen . . . is there anything I can do?

LORNA: Just go out for an hour.

ANDY: A minute, John. (*Closing the door and moving in*) Listen, you two . . .

LORNA: (*Furious*) Will you go for Christ's sake . . .

(ANDY *almost jumps out at the violence of the attack. Pause.*)

BILLY: (*Laughs.*) I've never heard you swearing like that before.

LORNA: It's not funny, you've nothing to laugh about. You've spoilt everything for me . . . you.

(*She slumps into a chair and cries a little.*)

BILLY: (*Frustrated*) What are you crying about?

LORNA: Why couldn't you just let things alone for once? How do you think Mavis and Pauline feel? They're not part of what happened and I'm sure they don't want to be.

BILLY: (*Coaxing*) Come on, Lorna . . . you know what I went through.

LORNA: What we all went through . . . and we've all tried to get over it. Dad's been through things too you know. He's come back to us . . . he's even staying out of his own house. You've ruined it all.

11. INT. BILLY'S AND PAULINE'S FLAT. EVENING

The meal is over.

MAVIS: I'll give you a hand to wash up.

PAULINE: No . . . please . . . I'd prefer to do it on my own . . . you two go on.

MAVIS: It was a lovely meal . . .

NORMAN: Yes, it was smashing . . . lovely . . .

PAULINE: Thanks.

(*Pause.*)

MAVIS: I'll . . . I'll just get ready.

(*She retreats into the bedroom.* PAULINE *starts to tidy the stuff on the table, prior to clearing it. She does this slowly in an abstracted, uninterested way.*)

NORMAN: Do you like nursing then?

PAULINE: Yes . . . I do.

NORMAN: I'm not much of a one for hospitals myself. (*Pause.*) Janet . . . Mrs Martin . . . that's Billy's mother like . . . she died up in the City.

PAULINE: Nobody likes hospitals in those circumstances.

NORMAN: No. (*Pause.*) Does he . . . Billy . . . does he ever talk about her?

PAULINE: Sometimes . . . not about her as such . . . just about her dying.

NORMAN: It happened at a bad age for him . . . for them all really.

PAULINE: I don't think there's a good age to lose your mother.

NORMAN: No . . . that's true . . . I remember my own . . .

(*He lets it drop, sensing no interest on* PAULINE*'s part. To his relief* MAVIS *returns.*)

Ah . . . you're ready?

MAVIS: Yes.

NORMAN: (*All business, putting on his coat*) If he'd been in we could all have gone down. (*Pause*) Right . . . we'll not be late . . . ah, see you later.

PAULINE: (*Going to the cabinet*) Oh, here . . . (*Takes out a key.*) Billy . . . got that cut . . . just to let you feel free . . . to come and go.

NORMAN: (*The emphasis on Billy not lost on him*) Great . . . thanks.

MAVIS: (*With a slight squeeze on* PAULINE*'s arm and a smile*) I'll see you later Pauline . . . we'll not be late.

(*They go. Pause.* PAULINE *sits, sighs, gazes into space.*)

12. INT. THE MARTINS' LIVING ROOM. EVENING

LORNA *is busy in the scullery.* ANDY *and* JOHN FLETCHER *are playing draughts.*

ANDY: (*Losing, and not too happy about it*) I knowed I should have took the black this time.

JOHN: You're the one always says we're not supposed to change colours in the middle of a set.

ANDY: Aye . . . I've no luck with black. (*Whisper, glancing towards the scullery*) Here . . . light one of them fags.

JOHN: (*Lights a cigarette, reluctant*) I don't want toul off.

ANDY: Don't worry.

(*Once* JOHN *has lit the cigarette, it is passed back and forth . . . glances at the scullery . . . being careful not to be caught.*)

JOHN: What's this new woman to you then?

ANDY: Eh? (*Thinks.*) She must be my sister-in-law . . . once removed, or something like that. She's a quare nice woman, mind. A qualified teacher too.

JOHN: She looked it . . .

(ANDY *gives him a look.*)

Nice . . . just the bit of a glance I got.

ANDY: (*Cautious, dropping his voice*) I'll never know what she saw in him.

JOHN: Sure women are that odd, you'd never know. (*Pause.*) I never thought she'd be as nice looking though . . . she's got a quare oul pair of sticks.

ANDY: He'll be wearing himself out (*Giggles*) going up with the blind one morning.

(*They start to chuckle.* ANDY *is smoking at the time and this brings on a fit of coughing. As* LORNA *comes in he tries to pass the cigarette to* JOHN, *but* JOHN *is studying the board.* ANDY *tries to throw the cigarette into the fire, but it lands in the hearth . . . damning evidence.*)

LORNA: So that's what you're at. Honest to God . . . you've no sense at all. You're worse than the youngsters. Do you want to kill yourself?

ANDY: I was just having a (*Coughs*) a couple (*Coughs*) a couple (*Coughs*) of (*Coughs*) puffs (*Coughs*).

LORNA: (*Picking the discarded cigarette from the hearth and throwing it into the fire*) Just look at the state you've put yourself in.

(*He spits into the fire. She is disgusted.*)

I think all the men in this house are mad. (*Turning on* JOHN) As for you . . . can you not wait to get the day out at his funeral? If you had the looking after of him you wouldn't be so quick to teach him bad habits.

JOHN: (*Sheepish*) I'm sorry, Lorna . . .

ANDY: Teach me bad habits? Do you think I'm a big youngster?

LORNA: Youngster, yes . . . big, no . . . and you've no brains either.

ANDY: (*Stung*) Oh, have I not. (*Starts to rearrange the board.*) Come on . . . we'll see who has brains.

JOHN: Ah, for . . . look . . . you've wrecked the board . . . and I was winning.

ANDY: Come on, young smartie miss . . . we'll see who has brains.

LORNA: I don't have time to play games . . . I've too much to do. (*Going back to the scullery*) No more cigarettes.

(ANDY *is seething . . . but beaten. Pause.*)

ANDY: Right . . . let's have this decider.

JOHN: We can't start again.

ANDY: Why not?

JOHN: Sure I'd near the other game won.

ANDY: Won what . . . are you soft in the head? Only she interrupted I'd have flattened you with my counter-attack.

(ANN *and* MAUREEN *enter.*)

JOHN: Counter-attack? I'm damned sure you'd no counter-attack. That's my game . . . two each . . . no, two– one for me. I win . . . it's my set.

ANDY: Your set my arse.

ANN: What are you two arguing about?

ANDY: You just mind your own business, madam.

MAUREEN: Oul stupid draughts . . . you're like two big babies.

ANDY: And we'll cut your clever talk.

LORNA: (*Coming in*) Stop being ignorant with the children.

ANN: I'm not a child.

MAUREEN: Neither am I . . . we're more sensible than those two.

LORNA: That wouldn't be hard. He's after near choking to death on a cigarette.

MAUREEN: Why, did he eat it? You're supposed to smoke it.

ANDY: In the name of Jasus. (*Scattering the board*) Am I going to be made fun of all bloody night? Away home, John . . . we'll play again tomorrow.

JOHN: (*Rising*) I'm playing no more at all unless I'm given that last game.

ANDY: Oh . . . is that all? Well if you're not playing again don't bother your arse coming back into this house again.

JOHN: (*Grabbing his coat*) I'd it all sewn up.

LORNA: Oh, for goodness' sake . . . will you two sit there . . . shut up and grow up.

JOHN: I'd the game won and he knows it.

ANDY: You'd nothin' won. If the game's won at that stage why do we bother playing till the end at all, eh?

ANN: Come on and have a game of ludo, Maureen. It's better than oul supid draughts.

MAUREEN: (*Starting to pick up the draughts*) Wait till I get these up.

LORNA: You shouldn't have to do that . . . leave it to them that threw them.

JOHN: Don't look at me . . . it wasn't me . . . I didn't do it.

ANDY: In the name of . . . (*Scrambling down on his hands and knees*) Look . . . they're easy picked up.

(*As* ANDY *scrambles on the floor,* LORNA, ANN *and* MAUREEN *look at* JOHN. *Self-conscious, he joins* ANDY *on the floor. The three girls smile at each other.*)

13. INT. BILLY'S AND PAULINE'S FLAT. EVENING

PAULINE *is washing up when* BILLY *arrives. He removes his coat, boots, etc. He expects her to come through to the living room, but she doesn't. In the end he goes in to her. She pays no attention to him.*

BILLY: I'm sorry Pauline . . . I . . . (*Pause.*) Where are they? (*Pause.*) I'd better . . . apologize . . . I just couldn't . . .

(*She moves past him to replace glasses in the cabinet.*)

It's a lovely night. (*Pause.*) I thought the four of us might take a walk. (*Pause.*) Is there . . . ah . . . I don't suppose there's anything to eat?

(PAULINE *glares at him. She takes a loaf, butter, knife, pot of jam, teapot, teabag, milk, sugar, cup, plate and each in turn she bangs down on the shelf for him. This done, she finishes off and returns to the living room, without saying a word.*)

(*Following her*) Ah, come on, Pauline . . . this is daft. (*Pause.*) If you're going to shout . . . shout. Throw things even . . . but not this. (*Pause. A little angry*) This is just bloody stupid.

PAULINE: (*Springing up and facing him*) Stupid, am I?

(*She slaps his face. They both stand, motionless, stunned. Pause.*)

BILLY: (*Quietly*) I'm sorry, Pauline . . .

(*He gestures, unable to say anything more. She collapses into his arms. They cling to each other, as if in desperation.*)

14. INT. THE MARTINS' LIVING ROOM. EVENING

ANDY, LORNA, ANN *and* MAUREEN *are there.* MAUREEN *has just risen and changed channels on the television.*

ANDY: Ah, turn it off altogether. There's nothing worth a damn on it.

(*She does so.*)

ANN: We saw Ian and Valerie up the gardens.

MAUREEN: He was pushing the pram and all, like a big cissy.

LORNA: There's nothing cissy about that . . . sure it's his baby too.

ANDY: That's not a man's job. You wouldn't have done it in my day . . . not in Belfast anyway. Englishmen started all that nonsense.

LORNA: I like to see a man pushing a pram.

MAUREEN: I'll bet you our Billy won't do it when Pauline has a baby.

ANN: (*Without humour*) I wonder will my da do it if Mavis has one?

(LORNA *and* ANDY *exchange glances.*)

ANDY: That's a marvellous night. It reminds me of nights in the Far East . . . just before an attack.

MAUREEN: Did you always have a bad chest?

(ANN *giggles.*)

ANDY: Not that sort of an attack. The Japs . . . dirty wee yellow buggers . . . crept up on you.

ANN: Did you scalp them after you shot them?

ANDY: (*Indignant*) We were soldiers . . . not savages.

15. INT. BILLY'S AND PAULINE'S FLAT. EVENING

BILLY *and* PAULINE *are sitting.*

PAULINE: I think it would be better . . . kinder . . . just to say you had to work overtime.

BILLY: They'll know it's a lie.

PAULINE: It'll not hurt as much as an inadequate apology.

BILLY: You know, I sat in the City Hall grounds . . . watching the pigeons . . . wondering if any of them knew what had happened . . .

(*He's very serious. She bursts out laughing.*)

What are you laughing at?

(*He looks a little hurt at first, but is infected by her laughter and joins in.*)

PAULINE: It sounds like something out of a picture.

(*Pause.*)

BILLY: Do you like my da?

PAULINE: I don't know. I didn't hate him on sight. He seems very timid, nervous.

BILLY: That sounds like something out of a picture. Have they went out drinking?

PAULINE: I think they just had to get out of here. They said they were going for a drink and a stroll.

BILLY: I'm surprised they came over at all. Imagine bringing anybody to Belfast for a holiday.

PAULINE: Don't be silly. It's more than a holiday. They're married. She's your mother . . . stepmother. It's only natural she'd want to meet you all.

BILLY: What'll I call her?

PAULINE: (*Shrugs.*) Mavis . . . I suppose.

BILLY: I'm glad you're on earlies . . . at least you'll be here when I come in.

PAULINE: Unless I go to the City Hall to try and read the pigeons' minds.

(*They laugh. Sound of the key turning in the lock. They stop laughing, regard each other.* NORMAN *and* MAVIS *enter.* BILLY *stands, self-consciously.* NORMAN *stops awkwardly too.* PAULINE *rises.*)

Billy, this is Mavis. Mavis . . . Billy.

(*They shake hands.* BILLY *mumbles greetings.*)

MAVIS: I'm very pleased to meet you, Billy. Your father's told me so much about you . . .

(BILLY *and* NORMAN *look at each other and then at the floor.*)

I've been looking forward to it.

BILLY: It's . . . ah . . . it's nice to meet you too. (*Pause.*) Congratulations . . . on the marriage. Look . . . sit down.

MAVIS: I'll just put my coat away.

NORMAN: (*Almost springing forward*) I'll do that.

(*He takes her coat and makes for their room.*)

MAVIS: (*Sitting*) I can't quite believe I've walked through the streets of Belfast. It's so quiet . . . and . . . ordinary. I was terrified before I came over.

PAULINE: You can go for weeks unaware of anything happening.

(BILLY *finds it hard to keep his eyes off* MAVIS. NORMAN *returns.*)

NORMAN: (*Ill at ease*) Listen . . . why don't I make a cup of tea, eh?

(BILLY *looks at him in amazement.*)

PAULINE: Not at all, Mr Martin, I'll do it.

NORMAN: No . . . no . . . I insist.

PAULINE: But you don't know where everything is.

NORMAN: Well, now's as good a time as any to learn, what?

MAVIS: Why don't you both do it . . . then Pauline can show you where everything is, and I can talk to Billy?

NORMAN: Perfect. (*Easier*) Come on Pauline.

(*They go and* PAULINE *is careful to close the kitchen door behind them.* BILLY *tries to find somewhere to fix his gaze . . . other than* MAVIS.)

MAVIS: As a matter of fact I was less frightened of the streets of Belfast than of meeting you all.

BILLY: I'm sorry about tonight . . . I had . . .

MAVIS: (*Cutting in*) I can understand. I don't suppose I know the whole story . . . but your father has told me quite a lot . . . and he didn't blame any of you. (*Pause.*)

BILLY: (*Uncomfortable, finding conversation difficult*) How did you meet my da?

MAVIS: My sister and her husband own a pub . . . I was helping out. Your father came in a few times and we chatted. It started quite soon after he arrived.

BILLY: Weren't you married before?

MAVIS: Yes. My husband was killed . . . in a road accident.

BILLY: Did you not have any children?

MAVIS: No . . . but I've always wanted some.

BILLY: Maybe it'll be second time lucky?

MAVIS: Yes . . . (*Regarding him*) Well, it has been. (*Pause.*) How long have Pauline and you been together?

BILLY: Five or six months . . . living together.

MAVIS: She's a very nice girl. Your father has taken a great liking to her.

BILLY: He doesn't know her very well.

MAVIS: No, but you can usually tell quite soon whether you like someone or not . . . can't you?

BILLY: I think it's better to get to know them before making up your mind.

MAVIS: You're very defensive.

BILLY: I've had to do a lot of defending.

MAVIS: It takes a big man to admit he's been in the wrong.

BILLY: It takes an even bigger one not to have been in the wrong.

MAVIS: Well, I'd like to start from now and not go back into all of that. I know it's difficult, but I think it's best if we can all just start again.

BILLY: We don't have to start again . . . we just have to start. (MAVIS *is aware of the put-down. They lapse into a rather uncomfortable silence.* NORMAN *and* PAULINE *re-enter with tea and buttered scones. It is served out in silence, weak little smiles and gestures, an awareness of the awkwardness all round.*)

NORMAN: We dropped into Lavery's there when we were out . . . that place never changes.

BILLY: No . . . I've been in once or twice with Uncle Andy.

NORMAN: I'm sure Lorna could have done without him landed on her.

BILLY: They're getting on very well. She likes him.

(NORMAN *just grunts. He resents the affection for* ANDY.)
He's not well.

NORMAN: He was never well.
(*Pause.*)

BILLY: He helps Ann and Maureen with their homeworks.
(NORMAN *looks at* BILLY . . . *trying to figure out if he's being got at.*)

NORMAN: Aye . . . well the schools give far too much homework anyway. I'm sure they're glad to be on their holidays.

MAVIS: I always believed in lots of homework when I was teaching. I think it's very important, especially if it encourages parents to get involved with their children's work. (*Pause. Realizing* NORMAN*'s discomfort*) Of course teachers can sometimes overlook, or be totally unaware of, the problems in the home.

NORMAN: (*As if to get himself off the hook*) You had to work overtime tonight then?

BILLY: (*Caught out*) What . . . ah . . . yes . . .

PAULINE: Yes, he had. It doesn't happen very often, so it's hard to refuse.

NORMAN: Aye, well you don't want to be refusing overtime. It's always a bit of extra money after all. (*Pause.*) Mind you, you missed a beautiful dinner. (*To* MAVIS) Didn't he, love?

MAVIS: (*Aware of what has happened*) Yes . . . yes, it was a lovely meal.

PAULINE: There'll be lots of other dinners before you go away again. (*With a smile to* BILLY) Maybe we'll have pigeon pie some night.
(*He smiles.*)

16. INT. BILLY'S AND PAULINE'S FLAT. MORNING

The next morning. PAULINE *and* BILLY *have gone to work.* MAVIS *and* NORMAN *are there.*

MAVIS: It's not going to work, Norman.

NORMAN: Of course it is. You worry too much.

MAVIS: It's often difficult to talk to people for the first time, but with Billy it's different. It's more than that.

NORMAN: I never expected Billy to be easy . . . too much happened between us . . . but in the end it's not up to him. (*She gives him a look that says it is.*)
Look, love . . . we're not committing a crime. It's the most natural thing in the world. I mean Billy doesn't even live there any more. He's got all he wants here.

MAVIS: I had hoped they'd ask before we even got a chance to put it to them.

NORMAN: But maybe they will . . . if we give them time. We can always wait a bit.

MAVIS: No, the sooner it's broached the better. We agreed on that last night . . . and in fairness to Lorna.
(*Pause.*)

NORMAN: Listen, in the end they're just youngsters . . . all of them. They'll do what they're told.

MAVIS: I don't want that. (*Pause.*) It all looked so simple from over there. Ann doesn't like me . . . I can sense that.

NORMAN: Doesn't like you? Rubbish. Ann's my girl . . . there'll be no problems with her. (*Pause.*) Anyway . . . I'd better get away over there.

17. EXT. STREET CORNER. DAY

ANN *and* JOAN *are there.* LORNA *and* MAUREEN *approach.* LORNA *is carrying a shopping bag.*

LORNA: We're just going down Sandy Row for a few messages. We'll not be long.

ANN: Is my da coming down today?

LORNA: I expect he'll be here sometime. I've left the front door open, and the fire's lit. Uncle Andy's still in bed. I'll see you later.

ANN: (*As* LORNA *and* MAUREEN *walk away*) Right, see you. (*Pause. To* JOAN) I'm going up to see my da, are you coming?

JOAN: Where?

ANN: Up to our Billy's flat.

JOAN: Away up there? But sure he'll be here later . . . and I thought you didn't like her?

ANN: I don't . . . but I'm not going to let an oul bat like that stop me seeing my da. (*Pause.*) I'm going anyway . . .

JOAN: I'm not going away up there. I've to tidy the house.

(ANN *walks off.*)

I'll see you later.

18. INT. THE MARTINS' LIVING ROOM. DAY

The fire is blazing, the room is empty. NORMAN *enters. He looks around. Once he establishes that there is no one there he lifts his wedding photograph from the mantelpiece. He takes it to the window and studies it.* ANDY *is heard moving around upstairs . . . coming down.* NORMAN *scurries back to the mantelpiece and replaces the photograph.*

ANDY: (*As he comes downstairs*) Oh aye, keep quiet . . . keep quiet . . . in case I hear you and ask for a sip of tea . . .

(*He enters on the end of this and is surprised and uncomfortable to find* NORMAN *there.*)

Oh . . . it's you . . . I thought it was Lorna . . . or one of the young ones.

NORMAN: Do you always lie in bed half the day and then roar your orders?

ANDY: I'm only asking for a drink of tea . . . that's not a big thing.

NORMAN: Well, don't bloody well ask me 'cause I'm not making you it. I'd see you in hell first.

ANDY: I'm not asking you. I can make it myself. Jasus, I'd be in a bad way if I'd to ask you to make me tea.

NORMAN: And I think our Lorna's enough to do without running after you morning, noon and night.

ANDY: Nobody runs after me.

NORMAN: Aye . . . well, my children aren't going to do it. (*Pause.*) Where are they anyway?

ANDY: I don't know.

NORMAN: Is it not near time you were thinking about going back to your own house?

ANDY: (*Flustered*) My own house . . . sure I sold that.

(*Sharp look from* NORMAN.)

The Housing Executive bought it . . . they'll be doing it up . . .

NORMAN: So you've moved in here permanently? To my house, and I wasn't even asked.

ANDY: Sure we all thought you'd moved out for good.

NORMAN: It's still my name on the rent book. I still send money to Lorna and bejasus I don't send it to keep the likes of you in tobacco and drink.

ANDY: I don't touch your money. I've me own. I pay my way.

NORMAN: And look at that fire . . . burning good coal in weather like this. Sure there's no need for that. I think while I'm over here I'll see the Welfare about getting you into a home.

ANDY: A home! I don't want to go into any home. Lorna promised me I could stay here.

NORMAN: Aye, well Lorna forgot this is my house. You've been here long enough.

ANDY: Aren't you going back to England? Hasn't Mavis got a big house? What do you want with this one?

NORMAN: Never you mind where the hell I'm going . . . or what Mavis has got. None of that's any of your business.

ANDY: I'm in and out of the hospital all the time.

NORMAN: Aye, well the next time you're in, stay in.

ANDY: I'm a sick man . . . you ask that wee girl of Billy's if you don't believe me.

NORMAN: My kids had enough of running up and down to hospital when their mother was bad. I'm not going to have all that again. Just get out of here. You've sponged on my kids long enough.

ANDY: What? What? Who're you calling a sponger?

NORMAN: (*Fiercely*) You . . . why?

ANDY: (*Pause. Quiet*) I'm not sponging . . . I'm giving my bit . . . you can ask Lorna.

NORMAN: I'm asking nobody nothing. I want you out. I don't like you, I never did. You were one of the ones who turned my own son against me.

ANDY: I what. . . ?

(*He sees the anger in* NORMAN*'s face and stops. After a moment's awkward silence shuffles into the scullery to make himself a cup of tea.*)

19. INT. BILLY'S AND PAULINE'S FLAT. DAY

The doorbell rings. MAVIS *emerges from the kitchen. She goes to the door and returns with* ANN.

MAVIS: Hello, Ann . . . it's nice to see you.

ANN: (*As they come in*) Where's my da?

MAVIS: He's gone down to your house. You must have virtually passed each other.
(*Pause.*)

ANN: I came up over the bridge. Where's Pauline and our Billy?

MAVIS: They're both at work . . . so we're all alone. (*Pause.*) Would you like something . . . tea, coffee, juice?

ANN: No.

MAVIS: No, thank you. You should always be good mannered . . . even to people you don't like.

ANN: I didn't say I didn't like you.

MAVIS: Not in so many words . . . and not to my face . . . but I'm not a fool.

ANN: (*Slightly wrong-footed*) I just didn't expect you to be married, that's all.

MAVIS: I see . . . and do you think you'd like me more if we weren't married?
(ANN *shrugs.*)
Or perhaps you thought that if you didn't like me you could have prevented us getting married. Is that it?
(ANN *shrugs again.*)
Why don't you say what you're thinking, Ann? It would be much better if you did.

ANN: (*Self-conscious*) I'm not thinking anything.

MAVIS: Oh, come on . . . cheer up. I'm not stealing your father from you. I want us to share him. We both love him. Look . . . I don't expect you to call me 'mother' either.

ANN: (*Sharply*) I wouldn't anyway.

MAVIS: That's fine then. I don't really expect anything from you.

ANN: Then why did you come over here?
(*Pause.*)

MAVIS: Well, to meet you all obviously. Your father wanted us all to meet and to get to know each other, and . . . well, who knows? I mean if I hadn't come over you'd have thought I was keeping him away from you, wouldn't you?

ANN: He could have come over on his own.

MAVIS: (*Stung*) We're married . . . I'm his wife . . . your stepmother . . . now that's not going to change so you had just better get used to the idea.

ANN: Why can't you stay here now then? Why do you have to take him back to England?

MAVIS: Because that's my . . . (*Pause.*) Your father has a job there. He's happy there.

ANN: You mean happy without us?

MAVIS: No . . . I don't mean that. (*Trying to break* ANN*'s gloom*) Ann . . . come on . . . smile, relax . . . for goodness' sake, child.

ANN: I'm not a child.

MAVIS: (*Thoughtful, rewarding* ANN *for a moment*) No . . . no, you're not.

20. INT. THE MARTINS' LIVING ROOM. DAY

ANDY *is finishing his tea.* NORMAN *is sitting, thinking. Neither speaks. After a moment* LORNA *and* MAUREEN *enter.* LORNA *and* NORMAN *exchange greetings.*

MAUREEN: Da . . .

(*She embraces and kisses him.*)

Where's Mavis?

NORMAN: She's up above.

MAUREEN: Have you fell out?

NORMAN: No, we have not.

LORNA: How was last night?

NORMAN: It was all right . . . when he finally presented himself.

LORNA: Did you not get a cup of tea?

NORMAN: No . . . I'm all right. I don't want any tea.

LORNA: Are you sure?

NORMAN: I'm fine.

LORNA: Did you get enough, Uncle Andy?

ANDY: Aye . . . aye . . . I'm all right.

MAUREEN: I'm away out . . . Da, would you give's ten pee?

LORNA: Maureen . . .

NORMAN: Let her alone . . . of course, love . . . (*Digging in his pocket he gives her a fifty.*) Here.

MAUREEN: Gee . . . thanks. Can I keep it all?

NORMAN: Of course . . . tear away there.

LORNA: (*To* MAUREEN) Do you see, you . . . don't you dare do that again.

NORMAN: She's all right . . . sure it's the holidays. (*With a quick glance at* ANDY *as* MAUREEN *goes*) Anyway, ampt I her father?

LORNA: What did you have to eat, Uncle Andy?

ANDY: I'd a piece of toast. I'm all right.

LORNA: What about your All-Bran?

ANDY: It'll do this morning.

LORNA: What have I told you about a proper breakfast?

(NORMAN *resents* LORNA*'s concern for* ANDY. *The door is rapped and opened.* JOHN FLETCHER *enters. He is taken aback when he sees* NORMAN.)

NORMAN: In the name of Jasus . . .

JOHN: Mr Martin . . . how are you?

NORMAN: I think before I go I'll put swing doors on there . . . make it easy for the crowds of you who use this house.

JOHN: I didn't know . . . it was Maureen . . . she told me just to come on in.

LORNA: It's all right, John. There's no harm done.

ANDY: I'm ready to go now anyway . . . I'll just get my coat. (*He does so.*)

JOHN: How's England then, Mr Martin?

NORMAN: I'm sure if you're interested you'll get the weather forecast on the wireless.

JOHN: Listen, Andy . . . I'll just stroll up to the corner . . . (*Going*) See you there.

(ANDY *gets ready, seething. He takes a coughing fit and spits into the fire.*)

NORMAN: (*Furious*) Go on, you filthy oul get.

ANDY: Aye, well, if I'm a filthy get, you're an ignorant one. (*At the door*) The sooner you're back in England out of the way the better.

(*He goes, banging the door.*)

21. EXT. STREET CORNER. DAY

JOAN *is there, smoking.* MAUREEN *arrives.*

MAUREEN: Where's our Ann?

JOAN: (*Gesturing*) There she's coming up the road. She was away up seeing your da and your new ma.

MAUREEN: She's English. You should call her 'mother'. And my da's up in our house. (*As* ANN *approaches*) Hey, Ann . . . you're bendy.

ANN: Don't you be so bloody cheeky. Is my da up there?

MAUREEN: Aye. (*Giggles.*) I told John Fletcher just to walk on in and he didn't know my da was there.

ANN: See you, you're a bad wee bitch.

MAUREEN: He wasn't in for very long. (*Giggles.*) Were you up seeing my . . . mother?

ANN: I was up seeing Save-us Mavis.

(*They laugh.*)

She talks dead posh.

MAUREEN: All English people talk posh.

JOAN: They do not . . . it's just the way they talk.

ANN: That's what we're saying.

JOAN: No, but I mean it's just the way they sound . . . it just sounds posh to us.

MAUREEN: What did she say to you?

ANN: Never you mind.

JOAN: (*Offering* ANN *her cigarette butt*) Do you want this?

ANN: No thanks. I've stopped smoking.

JOAN: (*Takes a few more puffs herself*) If you were a Fenian you'd be a saint.

MAUREEN: I'm bored with summer holidays. There's nothing to do.

ANN: It's better than school.

JOAN: You're dead right.

(ANDY *and* JOHN *approach.* MAUREEN *giggles.*)

ANN: (*Smirking*) I hear you popped in to say hello to my da, John?

ANDY: That's no laughing matter, girl. Not with a get as ignorant as your da. (*To* MAUREEN) Don't you ever do the likes of that again, young lady.

MAUREEN: (*Mock innocence*) What do you mean? I did nothing.

ANDY: Oh aye . . . you two never do nothing.

ANN: Hey, wait a minute . . . what did I do?

ANDY: Ah, for . . . come on, John. Let's get down the road . . . away from the whole damned lot of them.

(*They move on.*)

JOAN: Does John Fletcher still fancy your Lorna?

ANN: Well if he does too bad . . . she doesn't fancy him.

MAUREEN: He fancies Uncle Andy instead now.

(*They laugh.*)

22. INT. THE MARTINS' LIVING ROOM. DAY

LORNA *and* NORMAN *are sitting quietly.* NORMAN *has just told* LORNA *that he intends taking Ann and Maureen back to England with him.*

NORMAN: You could come too. We're not saying you can't.

LORNA: What would I do in England?

NORMAN: You'd be free to get a job . . . get a place of your own if you liked . . . a boyfriend.

LORNA: What about Uncle Andy?

NORMAN: To hell with Uncle Andy. I've told him it's time he got out of here.

LORNA: What? What did you do that for?

NORMAN: Because it is. I'm not going to send any more money to keep that oul get.

LORNA: What are you doing, Dad? First of all you're taking Ann and Maureen back to England. Now you're going to throw Uncle Andy out of here. Why? Why can't you just let us alone?

NORMAN: What are you on about? They're my youngsters. They need a father and mother.

LORNA: They've managed all right up till now.

NORMAN: That's as maybe . . . but it's time they had a proper home background.

LORNA: Is that the only reason you came over here? Is it just so that Mavis could get an instant family?

NORMAN: Now wait a minute, girl . . . just you watch your tongue.

LORNA: I thought I was gaining a mother, not losing two sisters Dad, we're happy here . . . don't spoil things again, please.

NORMAN: Oh, I see. So I'm still the big bad wolf, eh? I'm spoiling nothing. I'm offering my children a proper home.

LORNA: They've got a proper home here. They're happy here. All their friends are here. They'd hate England.

NORMAN: So you think they're better off here, with shootings and bombings and all the rest of it?

LORNA: They belong here, Dad.

NORMAN: They've never known anything else, that's all.

(*Pause.* NORMAN *rises awkwardly.*)

I'd better go on for now . . . Mavis is on her own.

LORNA: Are you going to report back that your mission has been successful?

NORMAN: There's no call for that.

LORNA: (*Rising, trying to control herself*) Isn't there?

NORMAN: What are you going to cry about?

LORNA: They're tears of joy . . . because you're going to take the kids off my hands. Thank Mavis for me. Tell her it's just what I've always wanted.

NORMAN: (*Threateningly*) Lorna . . .

LORNA: Oh aye, and you're getting rid of Uncle Andy as well. There's no end to your good works.

NORMAN: (*Exploding*) Now you listen to me, girl . . .

(ANN *and* MAUREEN *come in.*)

ANN: (*Taking in the situation*) Hello, Da.

NORMAN: Hello, love.

ANN: I was up seeing Mavis this morning.

(NORMAN *is slightly alarmed. He glances at* LORNA, *she drops her eyes.*)

NORMAN: Did she . . .

(*Pause. He is trying to read* ANN*'s face.*)

Was she pleased to see you?

(ANN *shrugs.*)

Listen, you two . . . look, come here.

(*He sits on the settee with one of them on either side of him.*)

How would you two like to come over to England?

MAUREEN: (*Thrilled*) England? Aye.

ANN: (*Glancing round at* LORNA) Do you mean for a holiday? With Billy and Lorna?

MAUREEN: And Pauline . . . and Uncle Andy?

(NORMAN *hesitates, aware of the implications of* ANN*'s question . . . a little unsure.*)

LORNA: No . . . Dad means just you two, and it's not for a holiday . . . it's to live there for good.

NORMAN: Lorna can come too . . . if she wants to.

LORNA: I don't.

ANN: (*Jumping up and moving towards* LORNA) I'm not going. I don't want to live in England . . . and I'm not going to live with her.

NORMAN: (*Angry*) 'Her' . . . who's 'her' . . . you're talking about my wife . . . your mother.

MAUREEN: Our Billy calls her . . .

LORNA: (*Cutting in*) Shut up, Maureen.

NORMAN: (*Glancing fiercely at* MAUREEN*, then back to* ANN) Mavis is your mother . . . and that's what you'll call her.

(*Pause. His anger has cowed them.*)

And another thing, you'll do what you're bloody well told . . . all of you.

ANN: (*Tearful*) Please, Da . . . I don't want to go to England.

NORMAN: If I say you're going to England you're going, and that's that.

MAUREEN: I want to go.

23. INT. BILLY'S AND PAULINE'S FLAT. EVENING

PAULINE *and* MAVIS *are there.* PAULINE *is just in. She is still wearing her uniform.* MAVIS *comes in from the kitchen with two cups of coffee.*

PAULINE: Cheers . . . this is great.

MAVIS: Busy day?

PAULINE: They're all busy. We'd a man died today . . . with the same thing Andy has.

MAVIS: Oh . . . so he really is sick?

PAULINE: Andy? Yes.

MAVIS: I didn't realize he was really ill. Norman gave me the impression he was malingering.

PAULINE: No . . . he'd give anybody that impression the way he goes on, but he is ill. Were you down in the house this morning?

MAVIS: No . . . Norman went down mid-morning, and he's not back yet. I can't imagine what's keeping him.

PAULINE: Maybe he's playing draughts with Andy.

MAVIS: I doubt that he'd be playing anything with Andy . . . there's no great love between them.

PAULINE: No. So have you been stuck in here all day on your own?

MAVIS: I don't mind . . . young Ann called up.

PAULINE: A visit from Ann . . . that's quite an honour. She must like you after all.

MAVIS: (*Smiling*) So you noticed too. No, quite the contrary . . . but it gave me the opportunity to put her straight on a number of things . . . mainly that I'm here to stay . . . in the family.

PAULINE: She'll come round. She adores Norman . . . it's probably jealousy.

MAVIS: I think there're all quite remarkable . . . considering what they've been through.

PAULINE: Yes . . . but they haven't all escaped unscathed, believe me.

MAVIS: You're telling me?

(*They laugh.*)

PAULINE: I'd better get started.

MAVIS: If you'd told me what you were going to do I could have had it prepared.

PAULINE: (*Thoughtful*) Do you know something . . . do you fancy being reckless?

MAVIS: I'm beginning to think I already have been.

PAULINE: Why don't we leave something for Norman and Billy

and go out and have a meal?

MAVIS: It sounds wonderful . . . but should we?

PAULINE: Why not?

MAVIS: Norman mightn't be pleased.

PAULINE: Good . . . it's best to displease him now . . . before he starts taking you for granted. Are you game?

MAVIS: Yes . . . yes . . . quickly, before we're caught

(*They laugh and go to get ready.*)

24. INT. THE MARTINS' LIVING ROOM. EVENING

LORNA, ANN *and* MAUREEN *are there.*

ANDY: (*Enters, beckoning*) Come on, John.

(FLETCHER *comes in. Nobody stirs.*)

Don't be overwhelmed by the welcome, they're just excited. (*Pause.*) Your da was going well in Lavery's.

(LORNA *merely looks at him.*)

Knocking them down rightly. Wouldn't think of asking us if we'd a mouth between us.

JOHN: He certainly looked like a man in a hurry to get drunk.

LORNA: If you'll excuse us, John, we're just going to have our dinner.

JOHN: Oh . . . aye . . . right . . .

ANDY: Houl on now . . . surely there's time for a game before it's ready?

LORNA: It's stew . . . it's ready now.

ANDY: Ach, stew's all right . . . sure it'll keep on a low light.

LORNA: It's ready now, and we're going to eat it now (*Going and holding the door open for* JOHN) without strangers gaping down our throats. (JOHN *goes.* ANDY *throws his coat on the floor in disgust.*)

ANDY: I'll have to check up now and see if there's anybody in this house that hasn't insulted that man.

LORNA: (*Very upset*) I've more to worry about than the feelings of John Fletcher. If you're so concerned about him away you go after him. Maybe he'll put you up when Dad throws you out.

ANDY: (*Realizing the state she's in*) It's not the end of the world . . .

you're not to get worked up on my account.

25. INT. BILLY'S AND PAULINE'S FLAT. EVENING

NORMAN *is there. He's been drinking, but isn't drunk. He has a handkerchief wrapped around one finger.* BILLY *enters.*

BILLY: (*Taking a moment to decide they're alone*) Where's Pauline and Mavis?

NORMAN: Out.

BILLY: Out? (*Pause.*) Is there anything wrong?

NORMAN: Aye.

(*Pause.*)

BILLY: What happened?

NORMAN: I near cut the finger off myself on that bastarding soup tin in there.

BILLY: Soup tin? (*Looking toward the kitchen*) What's going on?

NORMAN: It's on a low light. Lucky enough, I suppose . . . it's tomato.

(BILLY *goes in and checks around the kitchen.*)

BILLY: (*Returning*) Where are they?

(NORMAN *pulls a piece of paper from his pocket, hands it to* BILLY.)

NORMAN: They left that note.

BILLY: (*Reading it*) They've gone out for a meal? (*Pause.*) I thought I'd been forgiven for last night. I suppose this is Pauline's way of getting back at me.

NORMAN: Spiteful? That's the Fenian blood in her.

(BILLY *glares at him.*)

But what did I do? What sickens me is that they didn't even have the sense to open the tin and put the frigging soup in the pot. That's women for you.

BILLY: (*Resigning himself*) Will you want bread with this?

NORMAN: Aye. Does Pauline make a habit of this?

BILLY: No. Does Mavis?

NORMAN: How the hell would I know, we're only married. This is the first time . . . and the last.

BILLY: She seems to be a woman with a mind of her own.

NORMAN: Aye, well, she should remember that her mind's kept inside her head . . . and heads can be knocked off.

BILLY: You've been drinking.

NORMAN: So what?

BILLY: I thought you'd stopped?

NORMAN: Not at all. I still enjoy a pint.

BILLY: Aye . . . we'd better have this soup.

NORMAN: It's not much of a meal for you after a day's work.

BILLY: I'll survive.

NORMAN: If I go out and do a day's work I expect a proper meal at the end of it. That was one thing about your mother . . .

BILLY: (*Sharply*) Pauline works hard too. (*Pause.*) Did you say you wanted bread?

NORMAN: Aye, give's a few slices . . . just to dip in . . . no butter.

(BILLY *goes to sort things out.* NORMAN *follows him to the kitchen door, so that he can talk in to him.*)

I don't drink the way I used to. There's none of the oul fighting or anything . . . that's all over now. Mavis . . . (*Pause.*) That sort of thing's never going to happen again.

BILLY: Do you take salt?

NORMAN: Eh? Oh aye . . . no . . . not in tomato soup.

(BILLY *brings the stuff out on a tray.* NORMAN *follows him out again. They settle down to their soup.*)

You say Lorna and that other oul shite are getting on all right?

BILLY: Andy? Fine . . . yes.

NORMAN: I was thinking of telling him to go.

BILLY: Go? Where? Why?

NORMAN: Wherever the hell he likes . . . it's his problem.

BILLY: He's a sick man . . . genuinely very sick.

NORMAN: Sick, my arse. If he's that bad he should be in hospital.

BILLY: He's been in and out a couple of times.

NORMAN: She's her own life to lead. She can't tie herself down with the likes of him.

BILLY: Lorna knows what she's doing. Anyway, she wouldn't let him go.

NORMAN: It's my house . . . not Lorna's.

BILLY: Are you and Mavis going to move back into it?

NORMAN: That's not the point.

BILLY: (*Angry*) And what is the point?

NORMAN: (*Deliberately quiet*) The point is that I should be able to do what I like with what's mine.

BILLY: My advice is leave them alone.

NORMAN: (*Looking at him*) I didn't ask for your advice.

(BILLY *looks at him, shrugs and goes on with his soup.*)

I'm thinking of taking the two young ones back with me.

(BILLY *merely glances at him.*)

What do you think?

BILLY: Great, a holiday'll do them good. What about Lorna?

NORMAN: She doesn't want to come.

BILLY: If it's Uncle Andy, we could maybe do something. (*Smiling*) Unless you want to take him as well.

(*Norman responds with a glare. Pause.*)

NORMAN: It's not a holiday.

BILLY: (*Misunderstanding*) What do you expect in Belfast?

NORMAN: Not that . . . the kids. I'm not talking about a holiday. I'm taking them back for good.

BILLY: (*Staring at him until* NORMAN *meets his glare*) Have you said this to Lorna?

NORMAN: I put it to her this morning, aye.

BILLY: Did she agree?

NORMAN: I didn't ask her to agree . . . I just told her what I'm doing.

(*Pause.* BILLY *collects the dishes on to the tray.*)

Well?

BILLY: (*Looking directly at him*) I'm going to wash the dishes.

NORMAN: Is that all you can say?

BILLY: What else do you want?

NORMAN: An opinion for once.

BILLY: All right . . . my opinion is that you're wrong in just about everything you're planning to do.

NORMAN: Is that so?

BILLY: You keep on about Lorna leading her own life . . . that's what she does. The house . . . those kids . . . now Andy as well . . . that's her life.

NORMAN: That's no life for any young woman of her age.

BILLY: That's her life . . . and it's lucky for all of us it is. Now you're going to destroy it . . . everything.

NORMAN: Destroy nothing. Taking my kids to a proper home . . . with a proper mother and father . . . is that destroying? Is it?

BILLY: Da, you can't take people . . . two children, and give them to your new wife . . . as if they were ornaments. Why don't you and Mavis have a child of your own?

(*Pause.*)

NORMAN: Mavis can't have children.

BILLY: Well, why don't you adopt one then?

NORMAN: She doesn't want to adopt anybody. She's the mother of four children now . . . and if she wants two of them back in England, she's the right to have them.

BILLY: (*Angry*) And what about our rights?

NORMAN: You're living here with your girlfriend . . . that's your rights.

BILLY: What do you mean?

NORMAN: I mean you don't even live there any more. This is all between me and Lorna . . . not you.

(*They just glare at each other.*)

26. INT. THE MARTINS' LIVING ROOM. EVENING

LORNA *is just opening the door to admit* MAVIS *and* PAULINE.

LORNA: Goodness . . . are you two on your own?

PAULINE: Yes . . . we've come to take you out on the town.

LORNA: (*Not quite sure about* MAVIS) On the town?

PAULINE: We've been for a meal and now we've decided to go for a few drinks and make a night of it.

LORNA: Where's Dad . . . and Billy?

MAVIS: Your father didn't return after visiting here this morning. Pauline decided I'd spent enough time on my own.

PAULINE: We left them a tin of soup.

LORNA: Goodness . . . they'll not be too pleased.

PAULINE: They they'll know how women feel at times.

LORNA: (*Amused*) I can just imagine Dad and Billy stuck together with a tin of soup.

MAVIS: What time did your father leave here?

LORNA: (*Reminded*) Early . . . just after lunchtime.

MAVIS: As early as that . . . where on earth has he gone then?

(LORNA *keeps quiet.*)

PAULINE: We'll know soon enough. Get your coat, Lorna.

LORNA: Not tonight, Pauline . . . I couldn't go out . . . not like this.

MAVIS: We insist . . . and we'll wait until you get ready.

LORNA: And what about the kids?

PAULINE: Get ready . . . Ann's big enough to look after things for a couple of hours.

LORNA: And there's Uncle Andy. . . ?

MAVIS: Just go and get ready.

(LORNA *hesitates, thinking, attracted by the idea, looking from one to the other . . . then she goes to get ready.*)

LORNA: Right . . . I'll not be long.

27. EXT. STREET CORNER, EVENING

ANN *and* JOAN *are there.*

JOAN: I'd run away.

ANN: Run away . . . where to?

JOAN: Anywhere . . . there's places.

ANN: Would you come with me?

JOAN: Me? What for? Nobody's trying to make me go to England . . . I wish they were, I'd love to go. Think of all those lovely English fellas.

ANN: That's all you ever think about . . . boys.

JOAN: Places like Wolverhampton and all . . . I know a soldier from there.

MAUREEN: (*Just arriving*) Ann, you've to come in now. Our Lorna's going out.

ANN: Where's she going?

MAUREEN: I don't know. She's going out with Mavis and Pauline.

ANN: Is that oul bitch Mavis in our house?

MAUREEN: Come on . . . and Lorna says you've to come on your own. Nobody's allowed in.

JOAN: I don't want in . . . I'm lumbering the night anyway.

ANN: Who're you lumbering?

JOAN: That new fella at the bottom of the street.

MAUREEN: He's a drip . . . you'd lumber anything, Joan.

ANN: He's got a squint.

JOAN: Away to hell, he has not. That's deliberate . . . he does that with his eyes . . . it's dead sexy.

MAUREEN: Look . . . there's our Lorna at the door . . . come on.

ANN: I'll see you tomorrow.

(*They go.*)

MAUREEN: (*Shouting back*) Tell squinty I was asking about him.

JOAN: I'll give you a squint, wee girl.

28. INT. THE MARTINS' LIVING ROOM. EVENING

Sometime later.

ANN: Do you really want to go to England?

MAUREEN: Aye . . . it'll be brilliant.

ANN: And just leave our Billy and Lorna?

MAUREEN: Sure Billy's away with Pauline . . . and my da said our Lorna could come. She doesn't want to.

ANN: She doesn't want us to go.

MAUREEN: Well, I'm going. I'll be glad to get away from this oul street.

ANN: If you go, my da'll make me go too.

MAUREEN: Why do you want to stay in this oul hole?

ANN: What'll we do over there? They'll all make fun of us at school because of the way we talk. And the teachers'll pick on us and all.

MAUREEN: Sure they pick on us here and we don't talk funny.

ANN: Anyway they hate the Irish over there. We'll probably get beat up.

MAUREEN: They didn't beat my da up.

ANN: That's just because they couldn't.

MAUREEN: Anyway, we're not Irish . . . we're Protestants.

ANN: Don't be daft . . . we're Irish as well.

MAUREEN: No, we're not, I'm not anyway. Another thing, Mavis is English and she's our mother.

ANN: Will you stop calling her that. She's not our ma . . . our ma's dead.

MAUREEN: Well, now we've got a new one and I like her. I'm going to England with her.

ANN: (*Gazing at her*) You can go then . . . but I'm not.

MAUREEN: I don't care. Anyway my da'll make you go.

ANN: That's what he thinks. I'm not going . . . especially with her.

MAUREEN: You're just jealous 'cause she's married to my da and you think you're just Daddy's wee baby.

ANN: (*Totally furious, frightening* MAUREEN) You say that again, wee doll, and I'll break your face.

MAUREEN: All right, I didn't mean it . . . don't get excited.

29. INT. BILLY'S AND PAULINE'S FLAT. EVENING

BILLY *and* PAULINE *have just finished their dinner.* NORMAN *and* MAVIS *are out.*

BILLY: (*Sitting back, slapping his stomach*) Boy . . . that wasn't bad at all. I prefer tomato soup, mind you. A cup of tea now'll just round it off.

PAULINE: I had to dress your father's 'wound' before they went out.

BILLY: It's a pity he hadn't been opening it with his mouth.

PAULINE: Billy, that's an incredibly cruel thing to say.

BILLY: It was an incredibly cruel thing you and Mavis did, leaving me with him. Then taking poor Lorna out and getting her pissed.

PAULINE: She wasn't pissed . . . anyway, she needed the break.

BILLY: He'll take the kids away, you know.

PAULINE: What's going to happen to Lorna, once Andy has died and the girls have grown up and left?

BILLY: She'll just carry on.

PAULINE: Carry on doing what? I think it would be good for her if they left. She needs to get out of that house . . . get a job . . . start leading her own life.

BILLY: Did you talk about that to her last night?

PAULINE: Yes, we both did. Lorna had a row with your father, so her and Mavis were a bit embarrassed at first . . . but Mavis is really nice.

BILLY: If coming over to steal your sisters is very nice then I suppose she is.

PAULINE: Rubbish . . . do you want Lorna to end up an old maid? You tend to see everything in relation to your row with your father.

BILLY: My 'row' with my 'father' . . . is that all it was? You and Mavis know nothing about it. Just because he's putting on his big 'I'm a nice guy' act for Mavis you think we're exaggerating about it all.

PAULINE: I didn't say that.

BILLY: You don't have to say it. It's written all over your face. Stay out of this Pauline. It's something you don't understand.

PAULINE: Billy . . . I think Lorna needs to strike out on her own.

BILLY: Don't talk about her as if she's an idiot. You're all at that. Lorna knows what she wants. She can think for herself.

PAULINE: All I'm saying . . .

BILLY: Pauline . . . give it over. You've had a normal life. You'll never understand what it was really like for us.

PAULINE: You're becoming melodramatic . . .

(BILLY *rises, furious.*)

Where are you going?

BILLY: I'm going out.

PAULINE: Out where to?

BILLY: Mind your own business.

PAULINE: Billy, for goodness' sake . . . (*Rises.*) You're being ridiculous.

BILLY: (*Putting on his coat*) First it was melodramatic . . . now it's ridiculous. I'll go before you run out of big words.

PAULINE: Billy. . . .

BILLY: I need to talk to Lorna.

(*Pause.*)

PAULINE: Billy . . . I'm on your side.

BILLY: (*At the door*) Your trouble is that you don't even know

what my side is.
(*He goes.*)

30. INT. THE MARTINS' LIVING ROOM. EVENING

ANDY *and* LORNA *are sitting.*

ANDY: What do the youngsters themselves think?

LORNA: Maureen wants to go, Ann doesn't.

ANDY: The young one doesn't know any better. He's going well . . . taking the kids away and throwing me out.

LORNA: He'll not throw you out.

ANDY: Sure England's no place for youngsters. It's full of sex perverts and murderers.

LORNA: Mavis and Pauline seem to think it wouldn't be such a bad idea. They say I could get a job and lead my own life.

ANDY: Oh aye . . . and who's life do they think you're leading at the minute? I could laugh at that pair . . . one's never ever had childer . . . and the other one can't ever have them. A hell of a lot they know between them. (*Starting to tie his laces*) I'd better get ready and get down the road for a pint.
(BILLY *enters. Greetings are exchanged.*)

LORNA: Is Pauline not with you?

BILLY: No.

LORNA: Is there anything the matter?

BILLY: I wanted to talk to you about my da and the kids.

LORNA: I don't think there's much to say. He seems to have made up his mind.

ANDY: Do you know he's throwing me out as well?

BILLY: He'll not throw you out.

ANDY: Jasus I don't know . . . nobody seems too worried about what happens to me.

BILLY: Nothing's going to happen to you, he didn't mean it.

ANDY: Huh, I know your da better than that. Why'd he say it if he didn't mean it? (*Pause.*) Naw, you can't answer that. (*Pause.*) Anyway . . . I'm supposed to be going out for a pint. (*Prepares himself.*) You coming, Billy?

BILLY: No, go ahead.
(ANDY *goes.*)

(*To* LORNA) What are you going to do?

LORNA: What can I do? (*Pause.*) Ann says she's not going.

BILLY: Ann? I'd have expected it the other way round.

LORNA: She doesn't like Mavis.

BILLY: There's going to be a club for that soon.

LORNA: I like her, Billy. I can understand what she's trying to do. She thinks it's in my best interests in the long run.

BILLY: How do you feel about that?

LORNA: (*Shrugging her shoulders*) I just don't know what I'll do without them. I've no right to feel that way. They're not toys for any of us to play around with . . . but I can't imagine this place without them.

BILLY: Why didn't he just stay an alcoholic?

LORNA: He's right though. I mean he is their father, and now Mavis is their mother. What they're doing is right.

BILLY: It's all very well for Pauline and Mavis . . . they don't know what he was really like.

LORNA: I don't suppose Mavis would have married him if she'd known that.

BILLY: Maybe it's time we told her the whole story.

LORNA: Even if I could I wouldn't. She's the best thing that's ever happened to him . . . and the children are important to them. (*Pause.*) You know, last night, with Pauline and Mavis, I felt like a real woman for the first time in my life.

BILLY: (*Smiling*) I think you just enjoyed getting drunk.

LORNA: (*Smiling*) For all it took . . . I think I'd have felt drunk if I'd just been drinking water.

(*Pause. They sit there, still unthinkingly holding hands when* MAUREEN *enters.*)

LORNA: Where's Ann?

MAUREEN: She's away with Joan somewhere . . . following the bands or something.

LORNA: What bands?

MAUREEN: I don't know . . . a couple of bands that are out.

LORNA: D'you see that wee girl? That Joan one's a bad influence . . . she spends half her time chasing wee fellas . . . and the other half up the entries with them.

MAUREEN: (*Taking a ball*) I'm goin' up to the corner.
LORNA: Don't go any further now.
(MAUREEN *goes.*)
BILLY: Why don't we just tell them they're not going?
LORNA: We can't.
BILLY: Why not?
LORNA: Because it wouldn't make any difference.
BILLY: (*Angry*) It's not right. After all he's done he's going to walk back in and wreck things again. He shouldn't get away with it.

31. INT. BILLY'S AND PAULINE'S FLAT. EVENING

Quite late. NORMAN, MAVIS *and* PAULINE *are there.*
MAVIS: I saw my first Orange Band tonight.
PAULINE: Yes, I heard one earlier.
NORMAN: We should have come over for the twelfth. (*Aware of* PAULINE) Oh . . . I'm sorry, love . . .
PAULINE: (*Laughing*) Nonsense, I don't care. Many a time I've stood and watched them myself.
MAVIS: I was surprised at how young they were. I've always thought of them as dour, middle-aged men. Were you ever an Orangeman, Norman?
NORMAN: No . . . the oul fella was though. He never missed a twelfth at the Field.
PAULINE: Why did you never join, Mr Martin?
NORMAN: I don't really know . . . I thought about it once or twice . . . I just never got around to it. I'm not really a joiner. I remember taking Billy to the Field once . . . ach he was only a wee toddler at the time. A lovely sunny day . . . and I had to carry him most of the way there and back. The sweat was running down my back . . . he was on my shoulders . . . I thought he'd peed himself.
MAVIS: Maybe we'll come back for it next year . . . I'd love to see it.
NORMAN: Aye . . . aye we'll do that.
PAULINE: You can try carrying Billy on your shoulders again.
(*They are laughing as* BILLY *comes in. They exchange glances and*

fall silent. PAULINE *is looking quite apprehensive.* BILLY *has obviously had a few drinks.*)

BILLY: Hello, Pauline darling.

(*She responds.*)

Hello, Mummy and Daddy.

(*They look at each other and reply.*)

You're very quiet . . . I've always thought kidnappers would be noisy people.

MAVIS: I think you could use a strong cup of black coffee.

BILLY: What could I use it for, Mummy?

NORMAN: (*Rising*) Mavis . . . forget the coffee, we're going to bed.

BILLY: Of course, of course, go right ahead. Young honeymooners, we understand. Don't we, Pauline?

PAULINE: Shut up, Billy.

BILLY: Not that we've ever been on honeymoon ourselves. Well we can't get married you see . . . Northern Ireland . . . different religions. But we enjoy sex . . . don't we, love?

NORMAN: In the name of Jasus, boy . . .

MAVIS: Norman . . . you go on in . . . I'll see to Billy.

NORMAN: I'm bloody sure you'll not. You'll not put up with that . . . come on. The stupid wee frigger's drunk.

BILLY: You'd better do what Daddy says, Mummy. You wouldn't like him when he's angry.

PAULINE: (*Going and hanging on* BILLY*'s arm as a precaution*) Go on in, Mr Martin . . . Mavis. I'll see to Billy.

BILLY: See how popular I am, Da? They're afraid to leave us together, Mavis . . . afraid of something happening . . . you know? You see my last mummy . . .

NORMAN: (*Furious*) Now listen, you . . . I'll only take so much. Drunk or no drunk I'll break your bloody neck.

BILLY: You'll not throw me out on the street this time oul man . . . this is my place this time.

MAVIS: (*Getting in front of* NORMAN) Norman, will you please go to bed. I can take care of myself.

PAULINE: Please, Mr Martin.

BILLY: They're both on to you now, Da . . . I think we've got two sex maniacs here.

NORMAN: Pauline . . . are you going to shut that bastard up before I do?

(MAVIS *tries to steer* NORMAN *out, but he refuses to go.* PAULINE *tries to steer* BILLY *to the kitchen, but he resists.*)

BILLY: Away to bed, Da, the woman wants to finish her honeymoon. You never know . . . another little miracle . . . she'll maybe have one of her own and not have to kidnap my sisters.

(MAVIS *turns at this point, hurt. Before* NORMAN *can move she is across the floor and has slapped* BILLY*'s face, hard. The others are stunned, including* BILLY . . . *but* MAVIS *remains calm.* PAULINE *is crying.*)

MAVIS: I'm sorry Pauline.

(*Pause. They all stand, silent.*)

32. INT. THE MARTINS' LIVING ROOM. EVENING

LORNA *and* ANDY *are sitting. The others are in bed.* ANDY *is reading the paper.* LORNA *is gazing into the fire.* ANDY *puts down the paper. She doesn't stir. He looks at her for a moment. He has stopped smoking and is a little breathless.*

ANDY: This is what it could be like.

(*Pause.*)

LORNA: What?

ANDY: When the young ones are away and we're on our own.

(*Pause.*)

LORNA: Yea.

ANDY: Your da and me don't get on . . . but you know, love, he is within his rights.

LORNA: I know that.

ANDY: And like that woman'll make them a fine mother. He was lucky to get the likes of her, mind.

LORNA: I'll be the only one left in this house . . . I mean, the only one of us. It'll be strange.

ANDY: What'll you do with yourself?

LORNA: I'll try and get a job . . . anything.

ANDY: Aye . . . you're not to worry about me, mind . . . I'll be all right here during the day and all.

LORNA: I'll need a job anyway. I can't expect Dad to send money . . . with a wife and the two wee ones and all.

ANDY: If you and that other fella weren't so damned proud you'd have loads of money. I've toul you . . . it's there for you.

LORNA: Well, it'll still be there if we need it.

ANDY: (*Glancing at her*) I haven't taken a turn for a while . . . maybe I'm over all that now, eh?

LORNA: Uncle Andy, I'll make sure you're all right. I'm not going to neglect you.

ANDY: No, no, I'm not saying you will . . . not at all. You've kept your word all along. I've been well looked after . . . no complaints there.

(*Long pause.*)

LORNA: (*Emotional*) Uncle Andy, how am I going to say goodbye to those two?

ANDY: You'll come through it, love . . . Jasus, you've come through worse than that. (*Pause.*) I mean, there'll be a few tears, and why not . . . damn the shame in that. It'd be a bigger shame if there weren't.

LORNA: I know she'll be good to them . . .

ANDY: Of course she will . . . mind you, she'll be strict . . . she's a strong woman thon . . . there'll be no oul nonsense nor nothing.

LORNA: It's Ann I'm worried about. If she was keen to go I'd feel better about it.

ANDY: Huh . . . I wouldn't worry my head about her. Ann! Jasus that one'll survive the end of the world.

LORNA: (*Pause. Scrutinizing him*) You want them to go . . . don't you?

(*He takes a while to answer.*)

ANDY: I'd rather they'd leave me, than me leave them.

33. INT. BILLY'S AND PAULINE'S FLAT. NIGHT

PAULINE *and* MAVIS *are sitting.* NORMAN *and* BILLY *have gone to bed. It is late.*

PAULINE: He looks at me at times as if I'd betrayed him. He

wants me to hate his father with him.

MAVIS: Billy was the first one we should have spoken to. He just thinks it's the old Norman, bullying to get his own way again.

PAULINE: They've been very happy, you know. You just have to be in the house with them all to realize that.

MAVIS: Norman's missed them. It's hard to get it out of him . . . but I know.

(*Pause.*)

PAULINE: (*Yawning*) Oh . . . excuse me. I'd better clear up and get to my bed.

(*She rises.*)

MAVIS: (*Rising too*) You go on and I'll tidy-up . . . go on.

PAULINE: Thanks . . goodnight, Mavis.

MAVIS: Goodnight, love.

(PAULINE *goes. Pause.* MAVIS *starts clearing up. She is in the kitchen washing dishes when* BILLY *appears at the kitchen door. She turns and is startled.*)

Billy! Goodness, you gave me a fright.

(*Pause. He stands watching her.*)

Can't you sleep?

BILLY: You should've hit me harder . . . knocked me out.

MAVIS: I will . . . if you're ever as silly again. Would you like a cup of tea?

BILLY: Yes, please.

(*The kettle's already boiling. She makes the tea.*)

MAVIS: In here, or out there?

BILLY: Out here.

(*He takes his cup and they move into the living room.*

I'm sorry about that earlier.

MAVIS: Sorry just about what you said to me, or about what you said to your father as well?

BILLY: (*Looking at her*) About it all.

MAVIS: Why don't you tell your father that tomorrow?

BILLY: (*Self-conscious*) My da wouldn't know how to accept an apology.

(MAVIS *laughs and after a moment infects* BILLY.)

MAVIS: You two . . . honestly . . . if he was about twenty-five years younger, or you twenty-five years older, you could pose as twins. (*Laughs again.*) I've heard of some reasons for not apologizing but that beats them all.

(*They both laugh a little and then visibly relax.*)

BILLY: You must wonder what you've got yourself into?

MAVIS: Oh, I can cope. We'll all get to know each other much more quickly this way.

BILLY: Unless we fall out.

MAVIS: I don't believe in falling out, Billy. I believe in facing up to things and sorting them out.

BILLY: You know Ann doesn't want to go with you?

MAVIS: Yes. And if she gets any encouragement from you she'll be all the more determined not to go.

BILLY: She shouldn't be forced to go.

MAVIS: Come on, now . . . I'm sure Lorna and yourself have had to force her to do things she didn't want to do.

BILLY: That's different . . .

MAVIS: Oh yes, it's different. It doesn't involve your father appearing to win over you.

BILLY: I don't care about that . . . I care about Ann . . . and Lorna. What they want should be considered.

MAVIS: Billy, we're not absolute fools. There is no earthly way those kids can leave without Lorna, and them, being hurt . . . but I feel it has to be done.

BILLY: Why?

MAVIS: Don't shout. (*Pause.*) I believe we can offer them quite a lot. Also, it will ultimately be good for Lorna . . .

BILLY: How do you know that?

MAVIS: Because I'm a woman. Because I believe life has more to offer her than the burdens of child rearing, and looking after a sick old man.

BILLY: You've it all worked out, haven't you?

MAVIS: Not it all . . . I don't want to leave here having made an enemy of you. I'd like to think we could return and that Pauline and you'll visit us.

(*He just scowls.*)

Pauline would like to come . . . and she's big enough to do it on her own.

BILLY: Aye, well she'll probably have to.

MAVIS: You're getting aggressive again, Billy.

(*He rises with his cup.*)

BILLY: I'm going back to bed.

MAVIS: (*Rising*) Would you like some more tea?

(*He stops, regards his empty cup. turns to face her.*)

You can have a fraction of a cup. (*Smiles at him.*) I notice you and your father are great ones for that . . . a half, three-quarters, two-thirds . . . whatever you like.

BILLY: (*Unable not to smile*) Aye, all right.

(*He offers her the cup.*)

MAVIS: How much?

BILLY: Two-thirds.

(*They smile warmly at each other.*)

34. INT. A BAR. EVENING

IAN *is standing drinking. He bears the marks of a beating: black eye, scratches, etc. He appears gloomy, depressed.* BILLY *enters.* IAN*'s greeting is distinctly downbeat.*

BILLY: Hello, Ian.

IAN: Billy . . . what about you?

BILLY: I was supposed to meet my da here . . . have you seen him?

IAN: Your da. . . ? No.

BILLY: (*Looking around*) D'you want another one?

IAN: Aye, a pint.

BILLY: (*Orders.*) Has Valerie been thumping you?

IAN: I'd a row with her da.

BILLY: (*Looking at him*) Well, if you won I wouldn't like to see the state of him.

(IAN *doesn't respond to the humour.*)

IAN: I was going well, then I slid and the oul bastard stuck the boot in.

BILLY: What were you rowing about?

IAN: (*Bitter*) Ah, me and her's not getting on. If she could walk on her mouth she'd win the Olympic marathon . . . yap, yap, yap, never shuts bloody up.

BILLY: What business is that of his? (*The drinks are served.*)

IAN: (*Shifting, uncomfortable*) Ah, it was nothing.

(BILLY *keeps looking at him, awaiting the truth.*)

Ach . . . I was messing about a bit with Shirley. Valerie found out and toul her oul lad.

BILLY: So marriage isn't great?

IAN: Jasus . . . the biggest mistake of my life, I tell you. Sometimes I feel like just jumping from the top of that bloody ladder.

BILLY: You're still cleaning the windies then?

IAN: Aye. I'm on the dole as well . . . the double. Can't make enough at the oul windies.

BILLY: If you're caught that's six months up in Crumlin Road.

IAN: Would you write in and report me? Six months in gaol would get my bloody head showered.

BILLY: That bad?

IAN: Worse.

(TOMMY AGNEW *and* BIG DAVIE *enter.*)

Christ, here's her bloody da.

AGNEW: (*To* IAN) Hey you, get away home to hell out of this.

BILLY: (*Catching* IAN*'s arm as he makes to leave*) He's having a drink with me.

AGNEW: I'm not talking to you, Martin.

IAN: Look . . . it's all right, Billy . . . I'll run on.

BILLY: No, you'll not. I paid for that pint, you'll drink it.

AGNEW: Our Valerie's sitting waiting for him.

BILLY: She can wait another five minutes until he's finished his drink.

AGNEW: (*Uncertain. He looks at* BIG DAVIE.) This is none of your business, Martin.

BILLY: Listen, I'm having a quiet drink with Ian . . . so just get lost.

AGNEW: (*Another glance at* BIG DAVIE, *who smirks.*) You going to make me?

BILLY: Aye, certainly . . .

(BILLY *goes to him.*)

BIG DAVIE: Take it easy now, lads . . . take it easy. You're too quick to rise, Billy . . . like your da.

BILLY: I'm talking to Ian and I want that get out of the way.

BIG DAVIE: (*Sneering*) Two of yous and two of us.

IAN: Ah, Jasus, now, just a minute . . . look, Billy . . .

BILLY: Never mind. (*Facing* BIG DAVIE) This has bugger all to do with you . . . but you don't frighten me.

BIG DAVIE: I don't have to frighten you, son . . . I can just take you outside and take you apart.

BILLY: You can try it.

IAN: Ah, come on, now, lads. For Christ's sake, Billy.

AGNEW: (*Prodding* IAN) Shut you up or I'll drop you.

BIG DAVIE: Your da and me used to be good mates, Billy . . . but don't push me, son.

BILLY: Leave my da out of it. If Agnew doesn't move, I'm going to move him . . . and you can do what you like about it.

BIG DAVIE: You lay a finger on Tommy and I'll cripple you, son.

BILLY: Cripple me, I'll come back and beat you to death with my crutches. You know the only reason you two's in the UDA and not the Salvation Army is because you can't sing.

BIG DAVIE: You cheeky wee bastard . . . I'll leave you so's that Fenian nurse of yours won't recognize you.

IAN: (*Terrified*) Look, Tommy, I'd better get up to Valerie.

AGNEW: (*Pushing him back against the bar*) You stay there.

(BILLY *goes for* AGNEW *as* NORMAN *enters.*)

BILLY: I've warned you . . .

NORMAN: Billy . . .

(*They all stop.*)

What's going on?

(BIG DAVIE *is less confident,* AGNEW *looks frightened.*)

BIG DAVIE: What about you, Norman?

NORMAN: I'm all right . . . what's going on?

BIG DAVIE: Your wee fella here's getting ambitious . . . wants to have a go at me.

NORMAN: (*Looking at them*) Three of you?

IAN: It's not me, Norman . . . I'm with Billy . . . I'm just rushing home to the wife.

NORMAN: (*To* BIG DAVIE) So it's you and this shite? (*Pushing* AGNEW) Right . . . (*To* BILLY) Are you game, son?

BILLY: (*Looking at* NORMAN. *Pause. A slight smile.*) I'm game, Da.

NORMAN: (*Delighted*) Jasus . . . I wouldn't have missed this day for anything. Come on, son . . . outside, you two.

AGNEW: (*Reluctant*) Davie. . . ?

BIG DAVIE: Hold it, Norman . . . me and the young fella, no probs . . . you, on your own, just maybe . . . the both of you together . . . no way.

NORMAN: You backing down?

BIG DAVIE: Whatever way you want to put it . . . I'm not taking you two . . .

NORMAN: (*Grabbing* AGNEW) What about him?

BIG DAVIE: He's sorry he started all this and he's going to buy you a drink to apologize.
(NORMAN *releases him roughly.*)
Set them up, Tommy.

AGNEW: (*Disgruntled*) Four pints, is it?

IAN: (*Chirpy, moving beside* BILLY) Five.

NORMAN: (*To* BILLY) You settle for a pint, son?

BILLY: One?

BIG DAVIE: You bloody Martins . . . I'll buy the next one.

BILLY: Right.

35. INT. THE MARTINS' LIVING ROOM. EVENING

BILLY, NORMAN *and* IAN *are there.* LORNA *is making them tea.* BILLY *and* NORMAN *sport a bruise or two . . . but nothing serious.*

BILLY: (*Laughing, to* NORMAN) I thought Big Davie was going to cry when you hit him.

NORMAN: (*Laughing*) I've told you . . . never negotiate with the likes of them. Jasus, we learned that much from Chamberlain. Round here hard men are the ones who get the first dig in. It didn't take you long to finish oul Agnew.

BILLY: Ah, no problems.

IAN: I couldn't like . . . you know, da-in-law and all.

NORMAN: Ah, you'd have spoilt the Martin double act. We only wanted you to hold the coats.

(*They laugh.*)

LORNA: (*Coming in with the tea*) Honestly . . . (*Really delighted that* NORMAN *and* BILLY *are together*) Out fighting like silly big youngsters.

NORMAN: (*Indignant*) Big youngsters? Jasus, I'd love to see the big youngsters that could fight like us.

LORNA: I don't know what Mavis is going to say . . . or Pauline.

NORMAN: Davie's a sleekit big get. I knew what the game was. They'd've got us full of drink, then when they got half-a-dozen of their mates in we'd've been kicked round the streets. Davie seems to forget him and me were oul drinking buddies . . . I know his tricks.

LORNA: Yous put the heart across me . . . I thought you'd been fighting with each other when yous walked in.

NORMAN: Fighting with each other? If we'd been fighting with each other I'd've walked in . . . they'd've had to carry him in.

(BILLY *smiles.*)

In the name of Jasus.

LORNA: What's Valerie going to say to you, Ian?

IAN: She'll bate the tripe out of me.

(NORMAN *and* BILLY *laugh.*)

But sure I couldn't care less. (*Smirking, gulping his tea*) All the same . . . I'd better go . . . big day tomorrow you know . . . work . . .

NORMAN: You'd better get up early tomorrow . . . get away before Tommy gets hold of you.

IAN: (*Worried*) What? Sure I did nothing.

NORMAN: Neither did he . . . that's the trouble.

IAN: Aye, well, look . . . thanks. Thanks, Lorna . . . I'll be seeing yous.

(*He goes.*)

LORNA: More tea?

NORMAN: (*Looking at* BILLY, *considering*) Naw, love . . . we'd better be getting up to these two women. (*Rising, to* BILLY) Ready?

BILLY: Aye.

LORNA: (*Very happy*) It's really great to see you two together . . . even if you are hooligans.

NORMAN: The night's young yet . . . we could still have a row.

BILLY: Watch it . . . just because you stuck a lucky one on Big Davie . . . don't get too ambitious.

(LORNA *sees them out and they say their goodnights and go*.)

36. INT. THE MARTINS' LIVING ROOM. DAY

BILLY, ANN *and* MAUREEN *are there*.

ANN: Swear to God and hope to die.

BILLY: I will not. Look I've told you . . . (*Pause*.) We're friends now.

ANN: And when will you be over?

BILLY: For Christmas.

ANN: Christmas . . . that's not for ages.

MAUREEN: Will Pauline be with you?

BILLY: Of course.

MAUREEN: So will we get one dead dear present . . . or two cheap ones?

BILLY: We'll see how you behave.

ANN: Will Lorna and Uncle Andy get over too?

BILLY: Not all at the same time. It'll probably be too cold for Uncle Andy at Christmas. They'll go at Easter . . . or next summer.

ANN: Will you write to me, Billy?

BILLY: Aye . . . so'll Pauline and Lorna.

MAUREEN: What about me?

BILLY: We'll write to you too.

MAUREEN: I'm going to ask Uncle Andy to write to me.

ANN: Mavis says we'll have a room each.

MAUREEN: With desks and dressers and all.

(BILLY *is quiet, looking at them*.)

ANN: My da says I can have my own portable TV at Christmas.

MAUREEN: There's two toilets in the house.

(BILLY *is looking at the wedding photograph on the mantelpiece*.)

ANN: My da says he'll take us to the pictures and all.

MAUREEN: It's going to be just like having a real daddy and mummy.

37. INT. A PUB. DAY

The day of departure. BILLY *drinking alone.* IAN *approaches, carrying his drink.*

IAN: Billy . . . how's it going?

BILLY: Ian . . . all right.

IAN: I saw your da and the new missus. She's a bit of all right.

BILLY: Yea . . . she's great. How's Valerie?

IAN: Her. She's moved me into the back room.

BILLY: You still knocking Shirley off?

IAN: (*Looking around, cautious*) Mum's the word, eh? What–ever–you–say–say–nothing. Jasus, boy . . . when I think of the oul days . . . knocking about the corner, up the entry with Shirley. None of this bloody marriage lark.

BILLY: You're still up the entry with Shirley . . . so what's changed?

IAN: Everything's changed, mate . . . I didn't have to risk digs on the gub from Da Agnew before.

(BILLY *drains his glass.*)

Bit of advice, Billy . . . don't get married, mate . . . it's cat . . . no codding . . . (*Thumping his fist on the bar*) Barman . . . frig it, I'm going to get pissed.

(BILLY *looks at him and retreats.*)

38. INT. BILLY'S AND PAULINE'S FLAT. DAY

Later. NORMAN *and* MAVIS *are dressed up, their cases sit ready.* BILLY *and* PAULINE *are ready to go with them to the boat. They've just finished a meal.*

NORMAN: It doesn't feel like a week, does it?

MAVIS: It's a beautiful night for the crossing. I'm glad for the girls' sakes.

PAULINE: I think we'll fly over at Christmas . . . I hate the boat.

NORMAN: If you get a berth and get in and get your head down early it's OK.

PAULINE: I used to get seasick just on the swings, I'm afraid.

(BILLY *rises. They all watch him.*)

BILLY: Look . . . if nobody minds, I'd like to walk over . . . ah . . . I just feel like a walk.

(*Pause.*)

PAULINE: That's all right, love.

(*He goes.*)

NORMAN: (*Starting to rise*) Maybe I should . . .

MAVIS: (*Placing her hand on top of his*) No, love . . .

39. INT. THE MARTINS' LIVING ROOM

At some point in this scene a band has to be heard and build up until it enters the street. All are ready here. The girls' cases sit ready. LORNA *is gazing into the fire.* ANDY *and* JOHN *are playing draughts.* ANDY*'s mind is not on the game. He keeps glancing at* ANN, MAUREEN *and* LORNA.

JOHN: Your move.

ANDY: Aye . . . aye . . .

(*He makes a move.* JOHN *looks at him in surprise and then takes three or four of his pieces. When he looks back* ANDY *is gazing at the youngsters.*)

JOHN: Look . . . maybe we should leave it . . . you're off your game the night.

ANDY: Aye . . . aye . . . (*Rubbing himself*) It's the oul stomach . . . playing me up.

JOHN: (*Looking at the others*) Aye. I'll run on . . . we can start over again the morra . . . when you're feeling better.

(*On his way out he presses a pound each into the girls' hands.*)

Get a few sweets on the boat, girls.

(*They mutter their thanks as he rushes out embarrassed. Pause.* BILLY *enters. Pause.*)

ANDY: Where's the others?

BILLY: They'll be here soon . . . I just felt like a walk.

ANDY: The taxi'll be here at half-past.

(*They all sit glancing at each other. The band is close now and entering the street.* ANDY *rises and looks out of the window.*)

In the name of Jasus . . . look at that Ian fella . . . pissed out of his head . . . dancing about like a buck-edjit.

(MAUREEN *and* ANN *rise and look. They laugh and then go out to the street.* ANDY *follows them.* LORNA *and* BILLY *gaze at each other.*

There are tears on LORNA*'s cheeks.*)

LORNA: Are you and Dad still friends?

BILLY: (*Nodding*) Aye . . . Mavis even took photos of us.

LORNA: (*Smiling through her tears*) I'm glad that's sorted out . . .

BILLY: Aye. (*He takes the wedding photo and places it in a drawer.*)

(*The band is really banging out* Derry's Walls *by this stage.* BILLY *and* LORNA *go to the window together.* NORMAN, PAULINE *and* MAVIS *have arrived. They stand grouped around the door together, including* ANDY. *They are in view from the window.* BILLY *and* LORNA *remain inside.* IAN *is dancing around with* ANN *and* MAUREEN. *Pull back on Coolderry Street.*)

LORNA

Characters

LORNA
BILLY
ANDY
PAULINE
NORMAN
MAVIS
ANN
MAUREEN
JOHN
IAN
TOMMY
VALERIE
CLARE

Lorna was first shown on BBC Television in 1987. The cast was as follows:

LORNA	Bríd Brennan
BILLY	Kenneth Branagh
ANDY	Mark Mulholland
PAULINE	Julia Dearden
NORMAN	James Ellis
MAVIS	Gwen Taylor
ANN	Tracey Lynch
MAUREEN	Aine Gorman
JOHN	John Hewitt
IAN	Colum Convey
TOMMY	George Shane
VALERIE	Anné McCartney
CLARE	Dearbhla Molloy

Executive Producer	Keith Williams
Producer	Danny Boyle
Director	James Ormerod
Designer	Diane Menaul

1. EXT. COOLDERRY STREET, BELFAST. DAY

IAN *on ladder.*

VALERIE *walking towards* IAN. VALERIE *is carrying their son,* ERNIE, *and a large loaf of bread. As she reaches the foot of the ladder* IAN *sees them.*

IAN: Ernie . . . hey, Ernie.

(ERNIE *sees him, struggles, and the loaf falls into the bucket of water.*)

VALERIE: You stupid get . . . now look what you've done.

IAN: It wasn't me, love.

VALERIE: (*Shaking the ladder*) And who the hell else was it if it wasn't you?

IAN: Hey, hey . . . careful, love . . . you'll make the ladder fall.

(*He clambers down, and picks the loaf out of the bucket. Hands it to her.*)

VALERIE: What the hell am I supposed to do with that?

IAN: It's all right . . . it's sealed.

(VALERIE *hits him with it until slices fly all over the place.*)

VALERIE: If you hadn't ate the last bit of bread this morning, I wouldn't have needed any . . . you greedy oul shite.

IAN: But it was my breakfast, love.

VALERIE: You'd better get down to that shop and get me another loaf, and be bloody quick about it.

(*She pushes the bucket with her foot, sending the water all over his feet. He hops in pain, howling.*)

Get a bloody move on.

(*She turns away. The* POSTMAN *passes, smirks. We see him drop some letters into the Martin house.*)

2. INT. THE MARTIN HOUSE. DAY

The fire is blazing. LORNA *is in the scullery, preparing* ANDY*'s breakfast. She hears the rattle of letters in the hallway. She comes through and picks two letters up.*

LORNA: (*Calling up the stairs*) Uncle Andy! Are you up, Uncle Andy? Uncle Andy!

ANDY: (*Out of vision*) Aye, aye, aye . . . I'm up, I'm up . . . will you quit that roaring.

LORNA: I'm putting your milk on now.

ANDY: (*Out of vision*) Aye, I'm coming.

(*Suddenly there is a sustained burst of coughing from upstairs. The suddenness and ferocity of it startles her. She casts an anxious glance upwards.*)

3. *Andy's bedroom*

LORNA: (*Out of vision*) Uncle Andy! Are you all right? Uncle Andy!

ANDY: Aye, aye, aye . . .

(*He continues coughing, in some discomfort, and having some difficulty with his breathing. The coughing stops.*)

4. *The living room*

LORNA *listens. Pause. She opens the letters and starts to read them.*

5. INT. BILLY'S AND PAULINE'S FLAT. DAY

PAULINE *is sitting at the table, in her dressing gown, sipping tea.* BILLY, *dressed for work, is in the kitchen, packing sandwiches. He goes into the living room, ignores* PAULINE. *The atmosphere is very strained. They are not speaking.* BILLY *returns to the kitchen. He fills the flask, gets the milk from fridge. Exits kitchen. When he's gathered all his stuff together he leaves, without looking at her. She sits on just thinking.*

6. INT. THE MARTIN HOUSE. DAY

LORNA *and* ANDY *just look at each other. He moves to the table and sits. She pours his tea. Even the slight effort of moving to the table and sitting down renders him breathless again. He is at his worst in the mornings. There is a well-developed ritual whereby she lets him speak first, when he feels inclined to. He looks at the envelopes. Starts eating his breakfast.*

ANDY: Two letters . . . nothing for me then?

LORNA: No, not this morning. Maybe there'll be something in the second post. (*Pause.*) My Dad and Mavis both wrote.

ANDY: Jasus, they must have it. Why didn't they put the two in the one envelope and save the price of a stamp!

LORNA: Mavis was asking about you, and sends her love.

ANDY: (*Looking at her*) I don't suppose your Da sent me his?

LORNA: You know Dad . . . half a page.

ANDY: (*Hurt*) I suppose Ann and Maureen are busy . . . school and all.

LORNA: I'm sure they'll write soon. Maybe your letter to them went astray.

(*He looks at her. They both know that isn't true.*)

ANDY: I suppose like with Mavis being a teacher and all . . . I suppose she keeps them at it. Sure she's got them calling her 'Mummy' now . . . I'd love to see Ann's face when she's doing it. They sound like quare changed childer to me. Huh, Manchester . . . it might as well be another world. You know, I wouldn't be surprised your Da doesn't allow them to write to me.

LORNA: Mavis wouldn't let him stop them.

ANDY: Wouldn't you think they could have managed a wee letter between them? Jasus, they're the only nieces I've got.

LORNA: I'm your niece.

ANDY: Well, you're hardly going to be writing to me, are you?

(*Pause.*)

LORNA: You make sure and tell that doctor how breathless you're getting . . . and about the pains. (*Pause.*) Don't forget to tell him the coughing fits are getting longer.

ANDY: Not half as long as the nagging fits.

LORNA: I'm only telling you for your own good. One of these days you'll go into one of them coughing fits, lose your breath altogether, and that'll be the end of you.

(*They lapse into silence, while he finishes his breakfast.*)

7. INT. THE MARTIN HOUSE. DAY

LORNA *is in the scullery polishing shoes.* JOHN FLETCHER *enters.*

ANDY: Ah, John.

JOHN: Andy.

(JOHN *speaks to* LORNA *in the scullery and she replies.*)

JOHN: You said half nine, didn't you, Andy?

ANDY: Aye, I've to be there for half nine. Sit down there for a minute or two.

(JOHN *does so.*)

I'll not be long. Is it cold out?

JOHN: It's not too bad now, not too bad at all. (*Sits.*) Did you hear that shooting last night?

ANDY: Ach . . . cowboys playing themselves.

LORNA: It didn't mention it on the news this morning.

ANDY: There must have been nobody hurted. Sure those fellas never bother unless there's blood spilt. I think they cause half the trouble.

(ANDY *slips his feet into his shoes and* LORNA *ties them. As* ANDY *rises,* LORNA *goes and fetches his coat, scarf and cap.*)

LORNA: John, you make sure and tell them up there how bad he is.

JOHN: (*With a glance at* ANDY) Aye, I will.

ANDY: He will and me arse. I'm a bit breathless you know, not bloody dumb.

LORNA: I know you. If they ask you, you'll say you never felt better in your life.

ANDY: Aye, well sure neither I have.

(*He adjusts the cap she's put on.*)

LORNA: I'm warning you, Uncle Andy.

ANDY: Aye, all right, all right.

(JOHN *exits.*)

LORNA: What about your gloves?

ANDY: I don't want gloves. I'll keep my hands in my pockets.

LORNA: What happens if you fall with your hands in your pockets?

ANDY: In the name of . . . I'm not going to fall.

(*As* LORNA *and* ANDY *move towards the door, she dusts the back of his coat with her hand. They go.*)

8. INT. THE CONSERVATORY, NORMAN'S AND MAVIS'S HOUSE. EARLY MORNING

NORMAN, *ready for work, is checking some of the plants. He picks an insect off one, drops it on the floor and stamps on it repeatedly.* MAVIS *enters. She watches. He turns back to check other plants.*

MAVIS: Are you sure it's dead?

NORMAN: Cheeky wee blighter, just about to have a good feed to itself.

MAVIS: Maybe it doesn't have anyone like me to make breakfast for it. (*Going into the kitchen*) If you're starting at nine this morning you'd need to be moving. (*Pause.*) By the way . . . did you remember to post those letters to Lorna yesterday morning?

NORMAN: Mavis . . . (*Stops, quickly taps his pocket.*) . . . of course I remembered. I still think it's daft, you know, to send two letters to the same person, at the same address, in two different envelopes.

MAVIS: They were from two different people, Norman.

NORMAN: Even so, we could have saved the price of a stamp.

MAVIS: I don't know, sometimes I think you've never really left Belfast.

NORMAN: (*Plucking off a dead leaf*) Here now, we'll have none of this superior-English-woman bit. There's nothing wrong with Belfast.

MAVIS: I didn't say there was . . . but we do things differently over here.

NORMAN: All I was pointing out . . .

MAVIS: (*Smiling*) Norman . . . you're going to be late for work.

NORMAN: What? (*Checks his watch.*) Oh aye.

(*She offers her hand, which he takes, after wiping his own down his overalls and they leave the conservatory hand in hand.* MAVIS *and* NORMAN *pass* ANN *and* MAUREEN *in the doorway. The girls look at them.* MAUREEN *giggles.*)

ANN: That reminds me, I've to do an essay on *Romeo and Juliet.*

9. EXT. COOLDERRY STREET. DAY

LORNA: Get back early now – no sitting in the pub for the rest of the day.

(IAN *is working at the house next door to the Martin house.* JOHN *lets* ANDY *into the car, gets in himself and drives off.* IAN *puts clothes across rung of ladders and goes to the Martin house.*)

10. INT. CITY HOSPITAL OUTPATIENTS DEPARTMENT. DAY

JOHN *and* ANDY *are sitting. A middle-aged* WOMAN *sits on* ANDY*'s left.*

WOMAN: (*To* ANDY) Mind you, he was a younger man than you two. He used to near choke with the coughing . . . and anything like the pain he had to suffer, dear, dear.
(*Pause. She looks at* ANDY.)
God pity you, mister . . . my man died in agony. (*Shaking her head*) I pity you.

ANDY: (*Aside to* JOHN) In the name of Jasus . . .

NURSE: Mrs Smiley . . . Mrs Smiley, please.
(*The* WOMAN *rises and goes with the* NURSE. JOHN *and* ANDY *just look at each other.*)

11. INT. THE MARTIN HOUSE. DAY

IAN *is just finishing a cup of tea. The empty cup is in front of him. He takes out his cigarettes.*

IAN: Do you mind?

LORNA: No . . . go ahead.
(*He lights up.*)

IAN: No word of Billy and, ah . . . Pauline . . . getting married then?

LORNA: No, they seem happy enough the way they are.

IAN: Huh . . . they should stay that way then. (*Pause.*) What about your Da and the English woman?

LORNA: They seem very happy too.

IAN: Aye, everybody's happy but me.

LORNA: Go on . . . I'm sure you wouldn't change it for the world.

IAN: Wouldn't I . . . just give me the chance.

LORNA: You always seem bright and cheerful to me.

IAN: Aye, but that's not natural. You only see me when I'm working, and that's when I'm bright and cheerful . . . working! Anything to get me out of that house.

LORNA: How's wee Ernest?

IAN: Ernest . . . imagine the wee bitch giving my son that name . . . Ernie . . . gerny Ernie . . . that's what they'll call him. Ernie! He's great . . . he never stops crying and that still makes him the quietest one in that house.

(LORNA *smiles at* IAN*'s woes.*)
Me and her Da, we go out for a pint together now. Tommy's not a bad oul lad. We've both got the same problem . . . nagging wives. Do you know what we think? We think that her and her Ma rehearse, you know the way actors do? Valerie can nag non-stop for hours . . . she doesn't even stop for breath. Tommy says he thinks the oul doll can even do it under water. Sometimes I wish they'd both get what your Uncle Andy has . . . that might slow them down.

LORNA: Ian . . . God forgive you. If you could see Uncle Andy sometimes . . . you wouldn't wish that on your worst enemy.

IAN: I just have. (*Pause.*) Do you know she nags me and talks to the baby at the same time. (*Mimics*:) 'Who's Mummy's wee darling? . . . Will you get up off your arse and wash them dishes . . . There, darling, there mummy's wee angel . . . And then go and hang them nappies out before it starts to rain.' It's like living with one of them bloody ventriloquists.

12. INT. CITY HOSPITAL OUTPATIENTS DEPARTMENT. DAY

ANDY *is coming out of the doctor's consulting room. He wears his cap. The* NURSE *carries his overcoat, scarf, a letter and a prescription. She helps him on with his overcoat and scarf, as* JOHN *approaches. The* NURSE *hands* ANDY *first the letter, and then the prescription.*

NURSE: Take that to your doctor, and get that prescription as soon as you can.
(*She goes.* ANDY*'s demeanour shows that the news hasn't been good.* JOHN *just walks beside him, not speaking, but showing concern. As they reach the doors,* ANDY *stops.*)

ANDY: I don't think I can even walk as far as the car park . . . that doctor has me knackered.

JOHN: You sit down there . . . I'll nip up and get the car . . . it won't take me a minute.

ANDY: (*Slumping down*) D'you know . . . I think that Smiley woman was right . . . the oul bitch.

(*Concern on* JOHN*'s face, as* ANDY *lapses into a fit of coughing.* JOHN *goes. Hold on* ANDY.)

13. INT. THE MARTIN HOUSE. DAY

The living room.

PAULINE: I take it the news was bad for Andy?

LORNA: I think it was like you said . . . although he didn't really say much about it. He ran down the doctors and the Health Service . . . that's always a sign that things weren't good. He wasn't expecting any good news. I didn't think he'd go downhill so fast, neither did he.

(*Pause.*)

PAULINE: Are we going out tomorrow night?

LORNA: I'd like to . . . somewhere where there's a bit of life.

PAULINE: What about the nurses' disco?

LORNA: Why not.

PAULINE: Have you got the photographs for your driving licence yet?

LORNA: No . . . but I'll be in town tomorrow, I'll get them then. What's the test like?

PAULINE: (*Laughing*) It's a bit soon to be worrying about the test . . . you haven't taken your first lesson yet.

LORNA: John Fletcher's offered to give me lessons as well.

(PAULINE *looks at her.*)

I didn't tell him . . . it was Uncle Andy. I could have killed him. It was dead embarrassing. I just told him I'd do it with you first and see how it went.

PAULINE: It mightn't be a bad idea . . . it's the best way I know to kill any prospect of a relationship.

(PAULINE *rises to go.*)

LORNA: So what about us?

PAULINE: We'll be all right. I'll not forget I had to learn too. It's men . . . the way they go on you'd think they were born driving. (*Pause.*) Right, I must get back. I'll call about half seven tomorrow night.

LORNA: Here . . .

(LORNA *hands her the two letters.*)

Let Billy see those.

PAULINE: Right . . . (*Takes them.*) Thanks for the coffee.

(*She goes.*)

14. INT. BILLY'S AND PAULINE'S FLAT. DAY

BILLY *is at the table, a pot of tea in front of him. He's just finished his meal.* PAULINE *comes in, with bags of shopping. Takes off coat, places letters on the table in front of* BILLY. *He ignores them. She goes into the kitchen. She returns and sets the letters in front of him.*

PAULINE: Lorna sent those up, one from your Dad and one from Mavis.

(*Pause.*)

I'll be going out with Lorna tomorrow night.

(*No response.*)

We're going to a dance.

(*She sits at the table. He glances at her but says nothing.*)

It's a nurses' disco. We both want to go somewhere where there's a bit of life.

(*He ignores the taunt. Pours himself tea. Pause.*)

Am I not even going to be offered any?

(BILLY *pushes the teapot closer to* PAULINE. *He rises and crosses to the armchair. He just ignores her. Pause.*)

Billy.

(*Pause.*)

Billy!

(*He looks up at her.*)

I don't want to go on like this. I know everybody has rows and that would be all right. If we had big rows about something . . . we could get it off our chests and that would be that. We just niggle the whole time . . . about nothing very important. I know you're not enjoying it either . . . so let's either stop it, or break up.

BILLY: Fine.

PAULINE: (*???*) Which?

BILLY: Oh, you mean you haven't decided that too?

PAULINE: (*Angry*) You're the most irritating bugger I know.

BILLY: (*With a faint smile*) How many buggers do you know?

(PAULINE *glares at* BILLY, *but suddenly they are both laughing.* BILLY *rises and crosses to the table. With great ceremony he pours her tea.*)

PAULINE: Mavis is giving off about you not writing to her. Maybe I will. I could write to them . . . then you'd only have to add a few lines, or just sign your name.

BILLY: What do you want to do that for?

PAULINE: To keep in touch.

BILLY: So we write and tell them how we are . . . then Lorna writes and tells them how we are. They write and tell us how they are . . . then they write and tell Lorna how they are. Then we talk to Lorna, and we all tell each other how we all are. What's the point? It's all middle-class rubbish.

PAULINE: Writing letters isn't middle class. You and your Dad could probably communicate better by letter.

BILLY: My Da and me don't need to communicate at all. We've nothing to say to each other. Lorna'll tell him all he wants to know about me! Why should we sit down and make up things to say to each other?

PAULINE: Nobody's asking you to make up things. Say what you feel.

BILLY: I feel nothing. I know, I'll send him blank pages, eh?

(PAULINE *crosses to* BILLY.)

PAULINE: (*Exasperated*) Are you going to read the letters?

(BILLY *picks them up, examines them.*)

BILLY: No, I don't want to read them.

(*He pushes them away towards her.*)

PAULINE: (*Picking them up*) Do you want me to read them to you?

BILLY: What do you think I am, an idiot? Do you think I can't read?

PAULINE: I just thought it might be nice. (*She crosses to the settee and sits.*)

BILLY: 'Nice'! You could put that in your letters to them. 'Dear Mr Martin and Mavis, we play a little game called storytime. I read your letters to Billy.' Sometimes I wonder what you think I am.

PAULINE: I sometimes wonder what you are. You've got such a chip on your shoulder. I think you're afraid to be happy.

BILLY: Do you think reading my Da's letters to me will make me happy? I hate my Da.

PAULINE: Do you hate Mavis and Ann and Maureen?

BILLY: Ann and Maureen . . . What have my sisters got to do with it?

PAULINE: They live with him. They must love him.

BILLY: They didn't have any choice, did they? When he married Save-us-Mavis, he came over and took them . . . they were her wedding present.

PAULINE: I thought you liked Mavis?

BILLY: She's a 'nice' woman, if I can borrow one of your words, middle class like yourself . . . but she's also my Da's wife, so I've got nothing to say to her. I can go through the rest of my life without ever seeing either of them again, and I won't think I've missed anything.

(*Silence.* PAULINE *starts to clear the table.*)

PAULINE: Have you had enough?

BILLY: It's my dishes tonight.

PAULINE: Why don't we do them together? You wash and I'll dry.

BILLY: Then we can sit down and write all about it in a letter to my Da and Mavis.

PAULINE: Would you like me to help you?

(BILLY *rises and crosses to the table.*)

BILLY: I can manage.

PAULINE: That's not what I asked you.

BILLY: Sorry . . . it was a loaded, middle-class question. What was it again?

PAULINE: Forget it, Billy. You really are an irritating bugger.

BILLY: We've had this conversation before.

(*She continues to clear the table.*)

If it's my dishes, I'll clear the table, so just leave it.

(*She puts the plates down with a thud and goes and virtually flings herself into the settee.* BILLY *exits to kitchen.*)

How did Uncle Andy go at the hospital today?

PAULINE: I don't know.

BILLY: Didn't you call in with Lorna?

PAULINE: (*Out of vision*) Why don't you write and ask her?

BILLY: (*Returning to living room, angry*) I'll call in when I'm out . . . it's simpler.

PAULINE: You didn't say you were going out.

BILLY: I just have.

PAULINE: Where are you going?

BILLY: (*Shrugs.*) I might end up anywhere. A nurses' disco, who knows! If it's anywhere really exciting I'll write and tell you about it.

PAULINE: (*Angry*) Just give that a rest.

BILLY: Have I said something to upset you?

PAULINE: You didn't tell me you were going out tonight. I thought we were having a night in together.

BILLY: We'll do that tomorrow night if you like.

(*She lapses into an angry silence.*)

15. INT. THE MARTIN HOUSE. EVENING

Andy's bedroom. LORNA *enters, puts the hot-water bottle into his bed. She takes a small bottle of tablets from his bedside locker. It is almost full. She places two of the tablets and the glass of water on the locker. Goes.*

16. *The living room*

LORNA *comes downstairs.* ANDY *is seated at the fire.* LORNA *sits opposite* ANDY. *Pause.*

LORNA: A penny for them.

ANDY: Uh? Oh aye . . . I'd love a pipe.

LORNA: You know you can't have one.

ANDY: I know, I'm just saying . . . if it was a last request. Jasus, I'm dying anyway so it'll not make much difference.

LORNA: John went home early.

ANDY: His stomach. I think I sickened him . . . I bate him in every game.

LORNA: He's always bad with his stomach. Does he ever go and see about it?

ANDY: Jasus sure I don't know his business.

LORNA: He's your mate. He's very good to you.

ANDY: Aye, why shouldn't he be? Isn't that what being mates is all about?

LORNA: He's maybe got an ulcer.

ANDY: (*Looking at her*) You're very concerned about John.

(*She drops her head.*)

A bit of wind . . . a touch of the skitters. It's nothing serious.

LORNA: Many a man's been buried with less.

ANDY: In the name of . . . do you see yous women! There was an oul doll up in thon hospital the day, she'd me dead and buried in the few minutes she was sitting.

LORNA: You have to admit, they've buried healthier-looking men than you.

ANDY: Will you give over.

LORNA: It's only a joke.

(*Pause.*)

Pauline and me are going out tomorrow night.

ANDY: This is getting quite a thing with you two. Sure you were out last week.

LORNA: Uncle Andy . . . once a week.

ANDY: Where is it this time?

LORNA: A disco.

ANDY: Huh . . . if you want your feet amputated, why don't you get it done on the National Health? Can you dance?

LORNA: Of course I can dance. Why do you ask me that?

ANDY: I just wondered. I mean you never went out. How did you learn?

LORNA: I don't know. I think women just do it naturally.

ANDY: Like nagging.

LORNA: Did you never go dancing when you were young?

ANDY: Of course I did . . . but it was real dancing then. That kept the riff-raff out. Jasus, you only have to stand and wobble nowadays. There's no skill or grace with it any more. And look at the way they dress . . . like gypsies. In my day you had to dress respectably. You weren't allowed in unless you had a tie on.

LORNA: Anybody can put a tie on, that doesn't make you

respectable. My Dad never went out without a tie on . . . and he used to wreck half the pubs in the town.

ANDY: Aye, well your Da was your Da. There aren't many like him, thank goodness.

(LORNA *rises.*)

LORNA: Are you ready for your supper?

ANDY: D'you know, girl, I'm quite peckish.

LORNA: That's with all your gabbling.

ANDY: Do you know what I'd love? A bit of cheese. Do you have any cheese?

LORNA: I do. Do you want it in sandwiches, or on toast, or what?

ANDY: On sandwiches. Cut them intil squares, do you know crossways . . . and a good mug of tea. A nice strong mug of tea. Then a couple of them Marie biscuits and butter.

(*She just stands gazing at him, full of love. Pause. He looks at her.*)

What's the matter, have you no biscuits?

(*Pause. She just gazes.*)

What's the matter with you?

LORNA: (*Tearful*) Oh Uncle Andy.

ANDY: What . . . what is it?

LORNA: I love you.

(*He just gazes, dumbfounded.* LORNA *goes to scullery.*)

17. INT. THE PUB. EVENING

IAN *and* TOMMY *laughing.* BILLY *approaches.*

BILLY: Ian . . . Tommy.

IAN: Billy . . .

BILLY: You two are well on.

IAN: Jasus, Billy, it's medicine I tell you . . . if I didn't get out for a few pints I'd go mad . . . straight up.

BILLY: I called at your house.

IAN: Valerie's up at my Ma's.

BILLY: No, she's not . . . she was in the house.

(IAN *looks at him and then at* TOMMY.)

IAN: You're joking me . . . in our house? You mean my house?

(TOMMY *giggles.*)

BILLY: Your house . . . the house where you and Valerie live. The house where you sleep in the back room, except on your birthday and public holidays.

IAN: Oh shit.

(TOMMY *giggles.*)

BILLY: What?

IAN: Shit, mate . . . shit . . . the wee bitch's walked home on her own . . . I'm dead, tattie-frigging-bread.

TOMMY: Do you want another pint and a wee chaser?

IAN: Aye . . . aye . . . a double Irish, and a pint.

TOMMY: Billy?

BILLY: (*Amused*) No, I'm fine, thanks.

(TOMMY *orders drink, giggling.*)

What's wrong with her walking home on her own?

IAN: She made me swear I'd be up in an hour . . . martyrdom, that's all.

BILLY: She seemed in good form . . . brought me in, chatted, offered me a cup of tea. She didn't seem to be upset.

IAN: (*Shaking his head*) You don't know her, mate. You don't sleep in her back room.

18. INT. BILLY'S AND PAULINE'S FLAT. EVENING

The bedroom. PAULINE *is getting ready to go out. She is dressed and applying make-up, looking very well.* BILLY *comes to the door and stands for a moment, watching her. She notices him in the mirror. He turns and leaves the room.*

19. INT. THE MARTIN HOUSE. EVENING

The living room. ANDY *sitting.* LORNA *is almost ready to go out. She is raking the fire and putting coal on.*

ANDY: Sure I could have done that. You'll get yourself all dirty.

(LORNA *goes into the scullery.*)

LORNA: You're not to be shovelling coal. Get John to do that . . . and get him to settle it if he's going long before you go to bed. Get him to do the jar for you too.

ANDY: For Jasus' sake . . . I'm able to pour a drop of hot water intil a jar. Is the Billy fella coming down?

LORNA: He said he might. He could do the jar for you.

ANDY: Here, is that another new dress?

LORNA: What do you mean 'another' new one. To hear you, you'd think I was buying them every day.

ANDY: Well, mind you, there's been quite a few lately.

LORNA: I bought this one last Saturday. Do you like it?

ANDY: Aye, aye, it's a nice dress.

LORNA: (*Looking at him*) It's a nice dress . . . but?

ANDY: Nothing . . . nothing . . . just it looks a wee bit flashy.

LORNA: I didn't think it was me at all . . . but Pauline said it suited me. Do you not think it does?

ANDY: It suits you . . . oh aye it does . . . damn the thing wrong with it.

(*She looks at him.*)

Is there . . . ah . . . is there a fella on the go?

LORNA: There is one . . . but it's nothing special . . . we're just friends.

ANDY: Is he from round here?

LORNA: (*Amused*) No.

(*Pause.*)

ANDY: Is he from Belfast?

LORNA: Uncle Andy . . . you're fishing.

ANDY: Just curious. I might have til give you away, if your Da's not able.

LORNA: (*Laughing*) There'll be nobody giving me away. I've told you, he's just someone I'm a bit friendly with. He's a nice fella . . . we just dance. Then he usually comes and sits with us and we chat.

(ANDY *nods his head knowingly.*)

I don't even see him regular . . . he mightn't be there tonight. It's not a date or anything.

ANDY: No, no, I know what you mean. Sure I used to go to the dances myself.

LORNA: Did you have special dancing partners?

ANDY: I used to wear a wee dickie bow.

LORNA: You didn't!

ANDY: I did indeed . . . there was one lassie . . . Thelma . . . she always insisted that I should wear a dickie bow . . . distinguished she called it.

LORNA: Thelma . . . was she one of your special ones?

ANDY: Thelma McGimpsey . . . she was a coarse big Christian . . . but a lovely dancer. You'd never think to look at her, she could move like thon. She lifted me one night . . . ladies' choice . . . Jasus, the size of her lumbering towards me . . . but she was a lovely dancer.

LORNA: Did you ever go out with her . . . apart from dances?

ANDY: I took her for tea once . . . but sure off the dance floor she looked like nothing.

LORNA: Uncle Andy, that's a terrible thing to say. She was probably a very nice woman.

ANDY: She was nice enough. But when you took her out into the light, she wasn't the sort you wanted to be seen swinging on your arm.

LORNA: D'you see you . . . typical man. What's it matter what a person looks like, if they're nice?

ANDY: It mattered a hell of a lot to me in those days.

LORNA: Maybe if you hadn't been so fussy you wouldn't have ended up on your own.

(*Pause.* ANDY *gazes into the fire.*)

Sorry . . . I only meant . . . she might have made a very nice wife. (*Pause.*) Did you ever hear what happened to her?

ANDY: I never did . . . a big lump of a country girl . . . I'm sure she got married and raised a big family. (*Long pause.*) I'd quite a few of them running after me.

LORNA: Do you ever wish you'd got married?

ANDY: Ach, sometimes I think you're as well off on your own. Families is that much of a worry. Sure there's more miserable people married than enough. (*Pause.*) So, this fella . . . what do you know about him? Is he one of your own?

LORNA: He's a policeman.

ANDY: A policeman!

(*Sound of John's car arriving.*)

That's . . . that's . . . but you're just friends, you say? I mean you're not out in a car or anything with him, are you?

LORNA: Not yet. Don't tell me that you don't approve of a policeman?

ANDY: It's not that . . . it could just be a bit dangerous, that's all. Mind you, I never had a great deal of time for the peelers . . . still, you're just friends as you say . . . dancing partners.

LORNA: Pauline'll be here soon. (LORNA *gets up*.)

ANDY: She doesn't . . . I mean?

(JOHN *enters.* LORNA *looks at* ANDY, *shakes her head, goes upstairs.*)

JOHN: Where's she off to tonight?

ANDY: A disco dance. (*Pause.*) Can you dance?

JOHN: Naw . . . I don't think so.

ANDY: You don't think so! Jasus . . . if you can dance, you can dance, if you can't, you can't. I can't see what there is to think about.

JOHN: (*With a grin*) If I could I might go with her now and again.

(ANDY *just looks at him.*)

Do you think she'd let me?

ANDY: I don't know about that . . . But I think she'd lead you a right dance the same one. She'll never turn you away from the door, but she'll never close it up for the night with you on the inside.

(LORNA *comes downstairs, exits.*)

20. INT. DISCO. NIGHT

LORNA *and* PAULINE *to the foreground from bar, sipping a drink.*

PAULINE: Did you tell him you'd be here tonight?

LORNA: No, sure I didn't know I'd be here the last time I saw him . . . but I told him I might be.

(*They smile.*)

I don't care if he comes or not.

PAULINE: I thought you liked him?

LORNA: I do . . . I mean I enjoy a dance with him. I like his company, but that's it. Once you start going out with them they think they own you.

PAULINE: Not if you let them know the score at the outset.

LORNA: Look what happened with John Fletcher. He turned up one night with an engagement ring . . . right out of the blue.

PAULINE: I know . . . but look at John Fletcher, he's not what you would call a sophisticated person. I mean he was desperate. (*Pause.* LORNA *looks at her.*)

21. INT. THE MARTIN HOUSE. NIGHT

The living room.

JOHN *is sitting on his own. Draughts board set out on the table.* BILLY *enters.*

BILLY: John.

JOHN: Billy.

BILLY: Where's Uncle Andy?

JOHN: He's just out the back.

(BILLY *takes off his coat and sits.*)

BILLY: How's the car going?

JOHN: Grand. (*Pause.*) It's a right oul motor. It doesn't look much, but I've got my money's worth out of it.

BILLY: That's the main thing, isn't it?

JOHN: Aye. Lorna was saying she's wanting to learn. I said I'd take her out.

BILLY: I'm learning myself . . . in work.

JOHN: Aye, well . . . if you'd like to go out any time.

BILLY: Thanks.

(*Pause. Sound of* ANDY *returning.*)

ANDY: (*A little breathless*) Hello, Billy. I washed my hands, forgot Lorna was out. That water's cold. (*To* BILLY) Is Pauline away?

BILLY: Sure didn't she come down here to collect Lorna?

ANDY: Oh aye, she did, you're right . . . Jasus, the – oul head's going. You know I'll have to take a bit of sandpaper out to that oul sate. It's a bit rough . . . I thought I was going to get a skelf in my arse.

JOHN: (*Laughing*) It wouldn't do to get one there.

22. INT. DISCO. NIGHT

LORNA: Do you think I should go out with him? Bob, I mean.

PAULINE: It's entirely up to you. He's not going to stick around forever if you don't.

LORNA: Would you if it was you?

PAULINE: Lorna, I live with your brother . . . I'm not qualified to give advice about human beings.

LORNA: I sometimes worry about myself. I mean I don't really enjoy being out with fellas, I feel awkward, embarrassed, I just don't know what to say. (*Pause.*) I'm sure they think I'm stupid.

PAULINE: Don't be silly. Going out with men isn't compulsory, and when the right one comes along, you'll know, and you'll know what to say.

LORNA: What if the right one doesn't come along?

PAULINE: You'll have a quiet life.

23. INT. THE MARTIN HOUSE. NIGHT

The living room.

ANDY: Are you for waiting here until them two get back? Billy?

BILLY: I am not. I'll probably be in my bed fast asleep, before they come in.

JOHN: Sure if they get a couple of fellas you mightn't see them . . . (*Pause.*) . . . at all. (*Silence.*) Are you still working, Billy?

BILLY: (*Rising*) Aye.

ANDY: Stick to the work.

JOHN: Jobs are scarce.

24. INT. DISCO. NIGHT

A small lounge, close to the dancing area.

PAULINE: Are we going back in again?

LORNA: Yes, we'll just wait and hope those two morons have gone away.

PAULINE: What you have to put up with just for a night out! It's the assumption that you're theirs just for the taking that really annoys me. They just feel they have to go through their routine . . . men.

LORNA: Was our Billy like that?

PAULINE: I don't remember how your Billy first started chatting me up. It was the time Andy was on my ward. I think he used to ask loads and loads of questions . . . about Andy. And then one day I just realized he was actually chatting me up. (*Pause.*) I suppose it isn't easy, being a man.

25. INT. THE MARTIN HOUSE. NIGHT

The living room.

BILLY: You two play away at them draughts if you want to . . . don't let me stop you.

ANDY: Not at all . . . sure we've already had a couple of games. Here, put a wee shovel of coal on one of yous.

(*They both rise, but* JOHN *lets* BILLY *go and he rakes the fire out.*)

JOHN: There's nothing like a good coal fire.

ANDY: (*As* BILLY *puts coal on*) Maybe you'll fill a jar and put it in for me before you go, Billy?

BILLY: Will I do it now?

ANDY: No, it's time enough yet . . . before you go. Unless you want to go now, do you?

BILLY: No, I'll stay a while yet.

ANDY: Do you want to shove the kettle on?

BILLY: Aye . . . here, I'll tell you what . . . do you fancy a couple of bottles of stout?

ANDY: Jasus . . . now you're talking.

JOHN: (*Rising*) Why don't I nip down for them in the car? . . . it'll be quicker.

BILLY: (*Firmly*) I'll go . . . sure we're not in any great hurry.

(JOHN *sits again.* BILLY *puts on his coat.*)

ANDY: And Billy, a wee drop of whiskey. (*When* BILLY*'s gone*) Sit there, John, let him tear away. (*Pause.*) I don't think he likes that lassie out at the dances . . . for all their great talk about doing what they want to do.

26. INT. DISCO. NIGHT

PAULINE: I want things to work for me and Billy again, Lorna

... I really do. (*Pause.*) What about you ... what are you going to do after Andy dies?

LORNA: I don't know. I'd like to be able to just pack my bags and go.

PAULINE: Where would you go?

LORNA: I don't know. I just feel if I stay there I'll be stuck for good. I will end up with somebody like John ... just because it's easier. (*Pause.*) It's a bit frightening.

27. INT. THE MARTIN HOUSE. NIGHT

ANDY, BILLY *and* JOHN, *drinking. Half-a-dozen empty bottles sit. They are laughing at a story* ANDY *has been telling.*

ANDY: Jeez, he was a wild man, your Da, right enough.

JOHN: I'll never forget one night he hit me.

(*He looks at* BILLY.)

ANDY: (*Sad*) Ach, the past ... what's it matter. Funny, three or four bottles of stout and your whole life passes before you. I can remember the first time I met your Da at our house ... like a choirboy ... you'd think butter wouldn't melt in his mouth. But I knew him ... mind you, he was a good husband ... in the early days. They were a right happy couple when they'd just you and Lorna ... sure there wasn't a happier couple in the country. It all started to go wrong ... there was a bit of drinking, but nothing serious ... it was the time he went to England ... after he came back ...

BILLY: (*Drinking*) Just leave it, Uncle Andy.

ANDY: All I'm saying ...

BILLY: (*Fiercely*) I said drop it. (*Pause.*) I'll do that jar for you now ... then I'll have to get home.

(*He goes into the scullery.*)

ANDY: (*Quietly*) Jasus ... he's like his Da you know ... dangerous men, the pair of them.

28. EXT./INT. NORMAN'S AND MAVIS'S HOUSE. DAY

NORMAN *is dressed for the garden. He is watering the plants in the conservatory. He has a plastic bag sitting on the floor. Pause.* MAVIS *enters.*

MAVIS: Hello, love. (*Coming to be kissed on the cheek*) You're home early.

NORMAN: Aye . . . we finished a job and it wasn't worth while going to the other site today. Where are the young ones?

MAVIS: Swimming . . . I'll collect them in half an hour. (*Indicating*) What's in the bag?

NORMAN: Slug pellets . . . and pepper for the cats and dogs.

(NORMAN *crosses to* MAVIS.)

MAVIS: Norman . . . you'll have the neighbours complaining.

NORMAN: If they want pets they should learn to look after them. I caught that bitch from next door . . . got it a great boot up the backside. I nearly lifted it back over the fence.

MAVIS: When are you going to put the fine mesh up?

NORMAN: Aye, this weekend . . . but sure that'll not keep the cats out. (*Lifting his bag*) If this stuff doesn't work it's poison the next time.

(*He tramps off.* MAVIS *looks after him.*)

MAVIS: Would you like a cup of coffee?

NORMAN: (*Calling back*) Aye . . . bring it out. (*He spreads the pellets.*)

29. EXT. CLARE'S HOUSE. DAY

The exterior of Clare's posh, detached house in a prime residential area of Belfast. Her car is parked outside, and Billy's works van behind it. The DRIVER *exits and gets into the van.* BILLY *comes out with* CLARE.

CLARE: Thank you very much. It's a pity you can't do the tiling. It would be handy having the one person to do the whole lot.

BILLY: It's the sort of job that needs an experienced man.

CLARE: Yes, I suppose you're right . . . but you can manage the other?

BILLY: Yes, I can do that, no problem.

CLARE: Great . . . so I'll see you soon . . . Billy?

BILLY: Yes.

(*He goes and clambers into the van. It drives away.*)

30. INT. THE MARTIN HOUSE. EVENING

Andy's bedroom. He is in bed, much weaker. LORNA *puts his two pills on the locker, beside his glass of water. The bottle is just over three-quarters full. She puts it back in the locker drawer.* LORNA *is ready to go out.*

ANDY: Will you be late?

LORNA: No, I promise. John'll stay until I get back, in case you need anything.

ANDY: Need anything . . . you're treating me like a child. Billy and John . . . I don't need babysitters, you know.

LORNA: I just feel easier in my mind if I know there's somebody here. (*Pause.*) Would you rather I didn't go out?

ANDY: No, no, not at all . . . you run on . . . you need to get out.

LORNA: Why are you so gloomy?

(LORNA *sits on the bed.*)

ANDY: It's getting me down . . . I'm getting worse and worse. I can't even lie down properly. It's not living at all.

LORNA: Do you want me to ask the doctor to come and talk to you?

ANDY: (*With an effort*) Ah, never listen to me, love . . . I'm just a bit weary tonight.

(*Pause. She looks uneasy.*)

LORNA: I'll tell you what . . . I'll bring you up a wee cup of tea when I get back.

ANDY: That'd be great.

(*She goes. He lies for a moment, his eyes closed. He opens them. He looks at the tablets beside the glass. Pause.* ANDY *seems to reach a decision in his own mind. With a great physical effort he reaches into the locker drawer and removes a bottle of tablets. Clutching the bottle tightly in his hand, he sinks back, slightly breathless with the effort.*)

31. INT. THE MARTIN HOUSE. NIGHT.

LORNA *emerges from the scullery, carrying a tray with tea and sandwiches, etc., as a car draws up. Pause.* JOHN *knocks and enters.*

JOHN: How is he?

LORNA: He's sleeping. Sit down and take some of this . . . I made it for you.

(*He does so. Silence.*)

JOHN: He wants to die, you know. It's all he ever talks about now. Just no interest in nothing.

LORNA: I might ask the doctor to come out and have a word with him.

JOHN: I never thought he'd give up. If he goes what will I do?

(*Pause.* LORNA *looks at him.*)

LORNA: What will I do? (*Pause.*) Eat something.

(JOHN *reaches for a sandwich but stops.*)

JOHN: Sorry . . . Lorna . . . I'm just not in the mood.

(*Pause. They sit lost in their own thoughts.*)

How's the boyfriend?

LORNA: He's fine, fine.

JOHN: It's serious then?

LORNA: (*Quietly*) I haven't got a boyfriend . . . (*Pause.*) I'm sick of being dependent on people . . . and I'm sick of people being dependent on me. It's always like this in the end. I'd love to get away from this house . . . from this street. I'd love to be on my own . . . totally on my own . . . for a while anyway. I can't . . . (*Pause.*) I love him, John . . . but it's useless . . . what sort of life is he having?

JOHN: (*Hurriedly*) Aye, well. Thanks for the tea . . . sorry I couldn't eat anything . . . the oul stomach . . . it's bad again. (*Moves to* LORNA.) Look, Lorna. (*Pause. They gaze at each other.*) I'd better go up and sit with him.

(*He goes quickly upstairs. Pause. She sits a moment, cries. Sound of a car drawing up. Pause.* LORNA *goes into the scullery.* PAULINE *enters.*)

PAULINE: How's Andy?

LORNA: He's not well. John's up with him.

PAULINE: Are you all right?

LORNA: Yes . . . just feeling a bit sorry for myself.

PAULINE: Are you sure you're all right?

LORNA: I tried to talk to John Fletcher . . . he didn't understand. He just seemed to get uneasy and went. I just needed to talk to someone . . . but it's all right now. I didn't think you'd be down tonight. Are you all right?

PAULINE: Lorna . . . do you think your Billy's tired of me? It's just he's never away from that woman's house . . . painting for her . . . he says. I'm suspicious. He just seems so defensive . . . about her. At first he told me how nice she was . . . how nice-looking and all . . . and all about her lovely house. Now he says nothing. I think he's having an affair with her.

LORNA: Why don't you ask him straight out?

PAULINE: I'm afraid he'll tell me. (*Pause.*) Could you try and find out for me?

LORNA: He knows how close we are . . . he's not going to tell me anything he doesn't want you to know. Do you want to go out?

PAULINE: But sure you're going out.

LORNA: Come on . . . we'll go and have a drink somewhere . . . maybe you can give me a driving lesson.

(*They go.*)

32. EXT. COOLDERRY STREET. NIGHT

PAULINE *and* LORNA *exit house and get into car. They drive away.*

33. INT. THE MARTIN HOUSE. NIGHT

Andy's bedroom. ANDY *sleeps. He breathes quietly but with difficulty. The glass is now empty. His right hand is palm downwards on the bed.* JOHN *has been reading the evening paper, but now dozes. He wakens, a little uncertain of where he is. Looks at* ANDY. *Pause. Suddenly becomes aware of an awful silence.* ANDY *has stopped breathing. Gazes at him. Pause.*

JOHN: (*Frantic*) Andy . . . Andy! Ah, for Christ's sake, Andy, come on. Andy!

(*He lifts* ANDY*'s right hand. The empty pill bottle is under.* JOHN *drops his hand back. Stands back, gazes at* ANDY, *dazed.*)

34. *The living room*

JOHN *looking around, expecting to see* LORNA. *Stops. Realizes. Slumps into a chair. Covers his face with his hands and begins to sob, sobbing that becomes howling. After some moments he gets up and wanders out of the house.*

35. INT. RANGERS SUPPORTERS CLUB BAR. NIGHT

IAN *and* TOMMY.

IAN: She'd never agree . . . you know what she's like.

TOMMY: It's a lovely wee pup . . . great wee hunting dogs.

IAN: Aye . . . but she'd hunt me if I turned up with it. Hey . . . that's John Fletcher.

(*They look back.*)

What's he doing up here? He looks pissed. (*Going back towards* JOHN) John . . . what about you?

TOMMY: H'yi John.

(JOHN *doesn't stir.*)

IAN: Ignorant oul shite . . . Hey, John Fletcher, are you deaf?

TOMMY: Is he asleep?

IAN: (*Going closer*) John . . . are you all right?

JOHN: Are you all right? Naw, I'm not all right. Jasus, is there no peace to be had in this bloody town.

(*He staggers away. Pause.* IAN *and* TOMMY *look at each other, then start to walk away.*)

IAN: Didn't I tell you . . . oul shite's pissed. (*Turning and shouting*) G'on you grumpy old bollocks.

36. EXT. A CAR PARKED UP ON CHURCH ROAD ABOVE THE CITY. NIGHT

View down on the lights of the city. Cut into the car, BILLY *and* CLARE. *He has an arm around her. She is lying against him.*

CLARE: Beautiful, isn't it?

(*He grunts assent.*)

Don't you wonder what's going on? People down there . . . up to all sorts of things . . . living, dying . . . making love . . . giving birth . . . happy people . . . miserable people. (*Pause.*) You shouldn't be working down in that place . . . you should be out doing something better with your life.

BILLY: Does your husband know about you?

CLARE: Of course he does . . . we met before we got married. What is that supposed to mean, Billy?

BILLY: What time does he get home?

CLARE: He'll be home by now.

BILLY: And what are you going to tell him?

CLARE: The truth . . . that I screwed the fella who painted the kitchen . . . then ran him home, stopping to have a long cuddle on the way. (*Pause. Irritated*) What do you think I'm going to tell him? You needn't be afraid, he'll not beat you up . . . he isn't the aggressive type . . . or maybe he just wouldn't care enough.

BILLY: Why are so many people so miserable?

CLARE: Shit. (*Pulling away from him*) You're not exactly a barrel of laughs.

BILLY: Did you really need me to paint your kitchen?

CLARE: (*Starting the car*) I'll take you home.

BILLY: (*Reaching across and switching off the ignition*) I want to see you again.

CLARE: Maybe we should just leave things as they are. (*Starts car.*) I'll take you home.

BILLY: Drop me in Coolderry Street. I'll tell you where it is.

(*Car drives away.*)

37. EXT. COOLDERRY STREET. NIGHT

LORNA *and* PAULINE *in car. They get out. The front door of the house is open.* LORNA *enters house, followed by* PAULINE.

38. INT. THE MARTIN HOUSE. NIGHT

The living room.

LORNA *enters, goes upstairs.*

39. *Andy's bedroom*

LORNA *enters bedroom. She looks around as though she mightn't have noticed* JOHN. *She goes slowly to the bed. Calls for* PAULINE *and starts to cry as she does so. She sits on the bed, sobbing.* PAULINE *rushes in. Pauses. Eases* LORNA *up and comforts her.* PAULINE *leads her downstairs.*

40. *The living room*

LORNA *and* PAULINE *come downstairs.* PAULINE *sets* LORNA *into a chair at the fire. She tries to revive the neglected fire.* LORNA *is shivering.* PAULINE *drapes a coat around her shoulders.*

PAULINE: Sit there, love . . . just sit there.

(JOHN *enters.*)

Where've you been? Have you called the doctor?

(JOHN *shakes his head.*)

(*To* LORNA) Just sit there. I'll see to things, I'll go over the road and phone.

(PAULINE *goes. A pause.* JOHN *sits at the table.* LORNA *and* JOHN *sit, unable to find words to make contact.*)

41. EXT. COOLDERRY STREET. NIGHT

BILLY *approaching.* PAULINE *crosses back to the house. She sees him.*

PAULINE: Billy!

(*They meet, and enter house.*)

42. INT. THE MARTIN HOUSE. NIGHT

PAULINE *and* BILLY *enter. He goes straight to* LORNA. *Embraces her and begins to comfort her. She throws her arms around his neck, clings to him desperately, cries louder than ever, as if her heart is breaking.* LORNA *repeats* BILLY*'s name over and over between sobs.* JOHN *looks on, dazed and now aware of what he should have done and that it should be him she was clinging to. Slowly, sadly, he rises, and goes, unnoticed by the other two.*

43. INT. NORMAN'S AND MAVIS'S HOUSE. EARLY MORNING

The conservatory.

NORMAN: The selfish oul get. I don't know why they just didn't take him into hospital out of the way months ago.

MAVIS: Calm down . . . Poor thing.

NORMAN: (*As* ANN *and* MAUREEN *enter*) Poor thing! I should have thrown him out on his arse a long time ago.

ANN: Who? What's wrong, Dad?

MAVIS: Nothing. Are you two ready?

(*They nod.*)

MAUREEN: Who are you going to throw out, Da?

(ANN *nudges her.*)

MAVIS: Who say's 'Da', Maureen? Off you go.

NORMAN: Nothing, come on, do what you've been told, off you go to school.

(ANN *and* MAUREEN *go.* MAVIS *leads them to the door. Returns.*)

MAVIS: He must have been in a terrible state to do a thing like that. Lorna kept saying in her letters about how depressed he'd been recently.

NORMAN: He'd been depressed . . . does he ever think how depressed everybody else was, having to run after him?

MAVIS: You'll have to go over . . . for the funeral.

NORMAN: Sure, I couldn't stand the oul frigger.

MAVIS: That isn't the point. The man is dead. He was family and you should be there.

NORMAN: I can't have all this two-facedness. All this oul nonsense, making out somebody was great just because they're dead. (*He shrugs his shoulders.*)

MAVIS: I think you should be there . . . for the sake of Billy and Lorna. How must she be feeling? She'd grown very fond of him.

NORMAN: Oh, Jasus, aye . . . the oul bugger worked hard at that. He got the both of them round to his side.

MAVIS: Norman Martin, sometimes you're like a big schoolboy. Nobody tried harder than you did to turn those children against you. Never mind looking like that, it's true and you know it. Now you should be over there, supporting them. (*Pause.*) Maybe Lorna'll come back with you for a week or two.

(*Pause. He considers.*)

NORMAN: Maybe you're right.

MAVIS: (*Smiling*) Of course I'm right.

NORMAN: I hate bloody funerals. Do you know, my mother loved them. She'd have walked the feet off herself to go and watch a funeral. She used to drag me with her. And in those days people used to invite you in, to see the corpse before it was screwed down. Do you know what they say about the Irish? All their wars were merry, and all their songs were sad. You know they haven't gone mad over there . . . they were always bloody mad.

44. INT. THE MARTIN HOUSE. DAY

The post-funeral tea. BILLY, NORMAN, JOHN, IAN, TOMMY, *and* VALERIE *are in the room.* PAULINE *and* LORNA *are ferrying in refreshments.* NORMAN *is looking disgruntled.* VALERIE *is tipsy.*

45. *The scullery*

JOHN *is there.*

JOHN: (*Distressed*) I swear to God, Lorna . . . I hadn't a clue. I was just sitting reading the paper.

LORNA: You were supposed to be here looking after him.

PAULINE: Go into the living room, John.

(*Pause. He goes.*)

Lorna . . . Andy took his own life . . . on his own.

(PAULINE *enters the living room with teapot and brings it to the table.*)

IAN: Poor oul Andy . . . we'll all miss him.

VALERIE: (*Rises.*) You'll miss him, John. Why don't you come down to our house now and again for a wee bit of dinner. Ian could play Ludo with you.

JOHN: (*As* IAN *gives her a look*) It was draughts.

VALERIE: Not at all, our's is a warm house.

(LORNA *moves towards* BILLY *and* NORMAN.)

TOMMY: Here, you've had enough to drink. You've to wheel that pram home.

(LORNA *is with* BILLY.)

VALERIE: Da . . . go and get stuffed. (*As she pulls away she falls on* NORMAN*'s knee.*) Mr Martin . . . it was nice of you to come. Wasn't it, Lorna?

(PAULINE *crosses to* NORMAN *as* LORNA *brings in sandwiches.*)

I'm just saying, it was nice of your Da to come.

(LORNA *brings the sandwiches to the table.*)

PAULINE: Do you want tea, Valerie?

VALERIE: I'm saying John can come down to our house and play Ludo with Ian. Jesus, them's quare nice-looking sandwiches. I'm starving. I'd no lunch, with all the excitement of it all. Here, love, give's one of those. Here, Billy . . . you and your Da go for the posh women . . . are our sort not good enough for yous two? (*To* PAULINE) I used to fancy Billy.

(BILLY *moves to chair,* VALERIE *to settee.* PAULINE *moves to* IAN, *then to* JOHN, *then to the table.*)

TOMMY: You didn't bring the two young ones with you then, Norman?

NORMAN: Not at all . . . no, no . . . sure, they've their school to attend.

JOHN: He was very fond of them two. You could have let them come to their Uncle's funeral. School! It was their Uncle's funeral.

NORMAN: Aye, well, sure, as long as he was at it then, it wasn't a washout.

JOHN: (*Rising*) Now listen you . . .

(NORMAN *and* BILLY *rise.*)

BILLY: (*Getting between them*) . . . John, just calm down.

(LORNA *enters from scullery to table.*)

LORNA: Come on, John, have a wee bite to eat.

NORMAN: There'll be another bloody funeral if he's not careful.

BILLY: (*Angry*) Da . . . for God's sake . . .

PAULINE: Why don't you all stop drinking and have some tea and sandwiches.

(NORMAN *starts gathering the drink up, to deprive others.*)

LORNA: Dad . . . people mightn't have finished.

NORMAN: (*To all*) They've finished now, whether they like it or not.

VALERIE: (*From the settee*) Funerals and weddings are the only chance I get to have a quiet wee drink. It's you men that are drinking all the time, like that John Fletcher . . . you're an alcoholic.

BILLY: Valerie, give it a rest.

VALERIE: And he can go and find somewhere else to play his bloody Ludo. No wonder they were mates . . . two crabbed oul gets.

NORMAN: (*To* IAN) Here boy, would you either gag her, or take her away home to hell out of this.

VALERIE: Aye, will he . . . I'd love to see him try. Just because the oul frigger's dead . . . sure he'd never a good word to say about anybody. As for you Norman Martin . . . sure, you were never sober.

NORMAN: (*Pulling* VALERIE *up by the arm*) Right, come on . . . home to hell out of this . . . the whole lot of you . . . out . . . out.

(*Front door open. They all rise.*)

LORNA: Dad . . . there's tea and sandwiches.

NORMAN: They can get tea and sandwiches in their own houses.

TOMMY: (*Nervous*) Come on, Ian . . . grab her and come on.

VALERIE: (*To* IAN) Are you going to stand there and let him push me about?

IAN: Whereabouts in England are you, Norman?

VALERIE: Never mind that, you gormless get . . . hit him a good smack on the kisser . . . Da . . . you give him hand.

NORMAN: Hit me . . . them two . . .

BILLY: (*Getting between them and* NORMAN) Come on Ian, Tommy . . . you'd better go.

(IAN *tries to grab* VALERIE *and she swings at him.* TOMMY *grabs* VALERIE, *and with a gentle hand from* BILLY *gets her out.*)

VALERIE: (*Shouting back*) I always fancied you, Billy . . .

(*He closes the door on them.*)

JOHN: (*Ready to go*) I'll see you again, Lorna.

LORNA: Of course, John . . . call in any time.

JOHN: I'll see you, Billy . . . Pauline.

(*They respond. He and* NORMAN *just glare at each other.* JOHN *goes.*)

NORMAN: (*Moves to the table*) No wonder him and your man were mates . . . (*Reaching for a sandwich*) . . . I've never seen anybody ate as much at funerals.

LORNA: He was upset, Dad . . . him and Andy were very close.

(*She goes into the scullery.*)

PAULINE: I'll brew some fresh tea.

(*She follows* LORNA.)

NORMAN: (*At the fireplace to* BILLY) How's the work going?

BILLY: Fine . . . it's just work.

NORMAN: Lorna was saying you're doing bits on the side at nights.

BILLY: (*Unable to suppress a grin*) Yes . . . yes . . . it's always a few extra shillings.

(*He grins,* NORMAN *is puzzled.*)

NORMAN: And that's funny?

BILLY: What? No . . . no . . . I was just thinking about something else.

(PAULINE *returns and pours fresh tea.*)

NORMAN: Well you two . . . no sign of the first grandchild yet?

BILLY: (*Smiling*) Not yet.

PAULINE: We're not married, Mr Martin.

(LORNA *comes in and sits.*)

NORMAN: (*Embarrassed*) No, of course you're not . . . I forgot. (*Pause. To* LORNA) So what about you, Lorna . . . What are your plans now?

LORNA: (*Looks at him, considers.*) I'm thinking of joining the police. (NORMAN *just laughs, thinking she's joking.* BILLY *gazes at her.*) I'm not qualified for anything. The money's good. It'll make a change from nursing dying relatives.

NORMAN: (*Realizing she's serious*) Have you taken leave of your senses? You'll do nothing of the sort. You've a nice cosy wee home here . . . you could get a job in a shop or something.

LORNA: I don't want a job in a shop.

NORMAN: Maybe when you're over with me you'll see something you fancy.

LORNA: I've just told you what I fancy, Dad.

NORMAN: You're not serious, girl.

LORNA: Is it so terrible?

BILLY: (*Irritated*) Don't be silly, Lorna.

LORNA: Why is it silly? Why, when I for once decide on something I want to do, is it silly?

NORMAN: There's been enough daft talk for one day. At least that other edjit had the excuse of being pissed.

(LORNA *rises abruptly and takes stuff into the scullery.* PAULINE *follows.*)

Has she been talking about this for long?

BILLY: It's the first I've heard of it.

NORMAN: Maybe living with that oul get has drove her mad. (*They lapse into silence. Drink tea and eat. Pause.* LORNA *and* PAULINE *emerge from the scullery.*)

LORNA: I'm going to go up and pack . . . Pauline's going to give me a hand.

(*They go. Pause.*)

NORMAN: That other business you mentioned to me . . .

BILLY: That's what I was laughing at when you said about the wee bit on the side.

NORMAN: A bit on the side, so that's what you do when the painting's finished. So what do you do when the job ends?

BILLY: I don't know. She's got a husband, two kids.

(*Pause.* BILLY *rises to the table.*)

She's nice . . . I enjoy it . . . I mean . . . I'm not in love with her, or anything daft like that.

NORMAN: But you're not in love with Pauline either?

BILLY: We just don't seem to be able to talk at the moment. It's not one of us . . . we both seem to pick faults all the time. I'm just fed up with it. I'm thinking of moving out.

NORMAN: I like Pauline . . . I always did. Maybe you just need away from her for a while. The trouble is, this woman will probably just be the first . . . unless you can sort yourself out. Sooner or later Pauline'll find out. I know what I'm talking about. Why don't you move out for a while . . . move back in here with Lorna. Talk it over with Pauline . . . spend a while apart . . . then see how you feel.

BILLY: Does Mavis ever talk to you as if she thought you were an idiot?

NORMAN: Mavis doesn't think I'm an idiot . . . she knows it. But that's just Englishwomen.

BILLY: I'm going to go back to school . . . night classes.

NORMAN: If you can't beat them and all that.

BILLY: Have you ever thought of doing anything like that?

NORMAN: Me! Jasus, son . . . I get private tuition. You're not so bad . . . I've got three of them at me now. It's great to get back over here and be able to talk properly for a couple of days.

BILLY: Does she nag you about it?

NORMAN: No, no . . . Mavis doesn't nag . . . she just looks at me, as if I'm a dog that's just shit on the parlour carpet.

(*They laugh.*)

Here . . . let's go and have a civilized bottle of stout.

(*They exit.*)

46. MAVIS'S AND NORMAN'S HOUSE. DAY

The conservatory. MAVIS *is at home with* ANN *and* MAUREEN. *She is on the armchair cuddling* MAUREEN. ANN *beside them. They are upset.*

ANN: Why did he do that?

MAVIS: Well, he was very ill . . . he was dying, and I suppose he just wanted to do it with some dignity. He would eventually have just choked to death. It would have been very painful, and perhaps have taken weeks. (*Pause.*) I know it's sad, but I think it was also a very brave thing to do . . . and you must try and see it from his point of view. Now he wouldn't want you to sit about crying. That was the way he wanted it, and we have to respect that. Just try to think of all the fun you had with him. He used to make you laugh, didn't he?

ANN: He used to sit and spit into the fire.

MAVIS: Yes, well . . .

MAUREEN: My Da said he used to fart and blame the cat.

MAVIS: (*As they giggle*) Maureen . . .

MAUREEN: Sorry . . . my Daddy . . .

MAVIS: You two . . . I don't know.

MAUREEN: Are we allowed to stay off school tomorrow?

MAVIS: Why on earth would you stay off school?

MAUREEN: You always do when somebody dies.

ANN: That's right . . . for emotional reasons . . . we did when our Mum died.

MAVIS: Well, your Mum was different . . . she was closer to you . . . and you were there.

MAUREEN: She was Uncle Andy's sister.

ANN: That's right . . . we should at least be allowed to miss homeworks . . . to show respect.

MAVIS: There'll be no missed homeworks, and no missed school.

ANN: That's disrespectful.

MAVIS: It is not disrespectful. It could have happened at a weekend, or during the holidays.

MAUREEN: Our Uncle Andy wouldn't have done it then . . . he loved us.

MAVIS: Right . . . bedtime, I think. Your Dad will be back tomorrow and Lorna will be with him.

47. INT. THE MARTIN HOUSE. DAY

The living room is empty. Pause. The door opens. BILLY *comes in with his suitcase. He sets it in the middle of the floor, takes a good look around. Goes upstairs with the suitcase.*

48. MAVIS'S AND NORMAN'S HOUSE. EARLY EVENING

LORNA *in the conservatory/living room with* NORMAN *and* MAVIS. ANN *and* MAUREEN *are clearing up after supper. It is all done very properly.* LORNA *watches, amused at their care. She helps collect the plates. She exchanges smiling glances with* NORMAN *and* MAVIS. NORMAN *gives her a broad wink, and preens himself as a proud father showing off his well-brought-up offspring. When all is cleared away and the girls are washing the dishes,* NORMAN *goes off into the conservatory to tend his plants.* LORNA *and* MAVIS *move to comfortable seats. Pause. We can see* NORMAN *working down the conservatory. He wears boots as he has to go into the garden too.*

LORNA: I've never seen Dad so happy.

MAVIS: Half of his happiness comes from moaning about the way I've changed him.

LORNA: The girls have changed too.

MAVIS: You don't actually approve, do you?

LORNA: It's not you . . . I just thought . . . they just seem a little distant. I'm not sure what it is.

MAVIS: I suppose it's what two working-class Belfast children need to do, to fit into middle-class English society. (*Pause.*) It hasn't been easy for them, Lorna . . . for any of us. The adjustment has been painful at times. I know you expect them to react more to Andy's death . . . but it has been a long time since they saw him, in children's terms.

LORNA: Had you trouble with Ann?

MAVIS: I had trouble with both of them . . . they fed off each other. We had some real battles . . . I had to keep reminding myself that at heart I'm a tough Lancashire lass. There were times when I'd have found it easier to clear a rowdy bar. Your Father was very good. He didn't try the brute force and ignorance routine . . . he let us get on with it.

LORNA: Maybe I just expected them to be more the way they left.

(*Pause.* NORMAN *comes in.*)

NORMAN: Where's them new secatares, Mavis?

MAVIS: The cupboard beneath the sink. (*As he goes*) Norman!

(*He stops.*)

The boots, love.

NORMAN: Oh . . . aye.

(LORNA *giggles. He glances from her to* MAVIS.)

They're my carpets too, you know.

49. INT. THE MARTIN HOUSE. NIGHT

BILLY *sitting in the living room.* CLARE *enters from the back, washes her hands and comes through.*

BILLY: Are you all right?

CLARE: Yes . . . it's the first time I've ever used one.

BILLY: What . . . a loo?

CLARE: Silly. Oh, the fire's nice . . . it didn't take you long to light it. Is it one of those clever gas ones that looks real?

BILLY: No . . . it's real . . . but I cheated . . . I used half a box of firelighters to get it going quickly.

CLARE: Were you born here?

BILLY: In the front bedroom.

CLARE: Goodness. How many of you lived here?

BILLY: Oh, me, Lorna, my Ma and Da, two wee sisters, my four grandparents, two old uncles . . . and a one-eyed aunt . . . then we took in a lodger as well.

(CLARE *laughs and* BILLY *and* CLARE *embrace. He stops.*)

CLARE: What's wrong.

BILLY: Just thinking . . . nothing. Let's go up.

CLARE: Up? Can't we stay here in front of this nice fire? (*Sliding down on to the floor*) . . . come on . . .

(*He gets down beside her. Hold on them necking on the floor.*)

50. INT./EXT. MAVIS'S AND NORMAN'S HOUSE. DAY

LORNA *is on the phone in the hall.* NORMAN *is fussing around his pot plants in the conservatory.* LORNA *comes from hall to* NORMAN.

NORMAN: Did you get through?

LORNA: Pauline'll pick me up at the airport.

(*Pause.*)

NORMAN: So away again. Don't leave it as long to come back.

LORNA: You'll be opening a garden centre soon.

NORMAN: (*Weeding*) It's relaxing . . . gardening. (*Awkward*) Lorna . . . don't join the frigging police. Apart from the principle . . . you know. Listen, I can let you have some money if you wanted to train for something. In the police you'll just spend your life doing what somebody else wants you to do. You'll get no chance to be yourself.

LORNA: Dad . . . I want to do it on my own. There's money Uncle Andy left.

NORMAN: I see . . . you'd use his money, but not mine.

LORNA: Don't be silly . . . he can't use his where he is. You only have what you work for . . . and you've got a family to help support. (*Pause.*) There is something I want to ask you.
(*Pause.* NORMAN *looks at* LORNA.)
Would you let us bury Uncle Andy's ashes with Mum?
(NORMAN *gazes at* LORNA, *looking as if he might explode. Then he softens.*)

NORMAN: Aye . . . why not. Is that what he wanted, or was it your idea?

LORNA: He used to say he'd like to be buried with her . . . but he didn't think you'd agree.

NORMAN: The wee shite. (*Checking to ensure* MAVIS *isn't around*)
Do you know . . . I've a good mind to have him perfumed and use him as talcum powder.
(*They laugh. Suddenly they cling to each other, almost desperately.* MAVIS *enters.*)

MAVIS: Come on you two, that plane won't wait forever.

51. COOLDERRY STREET. EVENING

BILLY *comes up the street and enters the Martin house.*

52. INT. THE MARTIN HOUSE. NIGHT

LORNA *in the living room.*

LORNA: What's going on?

BILLY: I thought we could . . . you know, like the old days.

LORNA: Oh, did you? You thought you'd just move back in here, and I'd be your housekeeper . . . for as long as it suited you. Do you ever think of anyone else, Billy? Do you ever think of me? Does it ever enter your head that I just might want a life of my own? Well, do you know something? I can't wait to get out of this place. I can't wait to turn that corner for the very last time . . . and I'll never set foot in it again.

BILLY: It's still my home . . . I've still the right to stay here.

LORNA: Well, stay here then. Talk to Dad, I'm sure he'll agree to keep it on . . . but do it on your own. I didn't know you were planning to use this house as a base for screwing your woman friend . . . don't blame me because you got found out.

BILLY: I didn't think you even knew the word.

LORNA: No . . . people don't. People don't think I know anything, except how many slices there are in a big loaf, and how far it will go amongst five. You don't think of me as a real person.

BILLY: Don't be daft.

LORNA: I am not being daft. You've never thought of me as a woman. When I go out with a man you react as if I'm not normal. I don't swear . . . I don't drink . . . I don't have normal desires . . . I don't have a sex life . . . I'm only happy when I'm up to my elbows in soap suds . . . I'm not your maiden aunt you know, so for Christ's sake stop treating me as if I am.

BILLY: (*Rising*) I'm going down for a few pints.

LORNA: Don't . . . that's what Dad used to do. That's what the old Martin men used to do. Pull yourself together, Billy. I'm not going to be here to run back to any more . . . help me . . . stand on your own two feet . . . live your own life and let me get on with mine.

(LORNA *exits to scullery.*)

53. INT. THE MARTIN HOUSE. DAY

PAULINE *and* LORNA *are in the living room, packing and organizing the furniture removal.*

54. EXT. COOLDERRY STREET. DAY

A large van, two-thirds full of furniture, is parked outside the Martin house. The windows are whitened on the inside. BILLY, IAN *and*

TOMMY *are moving* LORNA*'s stuff.* BILLY *and* IAN *have the settee lodged in the doorway.* TOMMY *is directing operations from the street.*

TOMMY: No, no, no . . . take it back in and twist it round. It has to be upended. Ian . . . drop your end down.

IAN: (*Yelping with pain*) Ah . . . my frigging finger . . . houl on, Billy . . . Jasus.

TOMMY: Here . . . (*Pulling* IAN *away*) . . . let me.

BILLY: You get your chamois, Ian, and wipe the windscreen of the van.

(*Laughter. Pull out on street, as* TOMMY *and* BILLY *emerge with the settee.* JOHN *passes down on the far side of the street. He stops to stare. Pause. Moves on.*)

55. INT. MAVIS'S AND NORMAN'S HOUSE. NIGHT

The conservatory in darkness. NORMAN *is at the far end, looking out.* MAVIS *enters and switches on the lights.*

MAVIS: Norman . . . what are you doing?

NORMAN: Just thinking . . . Lorna rang . . . she's moved . . . She's just a few odds and ends to collect tomorrow. She's in her new flat tonight. (*Pause.*) It's empty tonight . . . I can see it, you know. Jasus, the nights I tramped up that wee street . . . or staggered and fell up it . . . there's no light on tonight.

MAVIS: What are Ann and Maureen up to?

NORMAN: Ach, just a wee notion I took . . . for a bit of tea and toast. A Coolderry Street supper, we did some living in that wee street.

(MAVIS *puts an arm around his waist. They enter living room.*)

56. EXT. COOLDERRY STREET. NIGHT

The windows of the Martin house are whitened. JOHN *staggers up the street. He starts banging on the door.*

JOHN: Andy . . . Andy . . . come on, you oul bugger, let me in. Andy, for Christ's sake, Andy . . . come on, open the door . . . just for a minute . . . just open the door for a minute.

57. INT. THE MARTIN HOUSE. NIGHT.

LORNA *is standing in Andy's bedroom, listening. Two bags sit at her feet, with some of Andy's stuff in one of them.*

58. EXT. THE MARTIN HOUSE. NIGHT

JOHN: Andy . . . (*Conversational*) . . . are you in, Andy? Come here . . . here . . . see, I thought you were joking . . . I thought it was only a wee joke . . . I didn't think you'd ever do that, you silly oul bastard. (*Pause.*) Come on. Let me in . . . Andy . . . Andy . . .

(*He fumbles the name over and over, crying drunkenly. Pull back, to show* JOHN *propped up against the door.* TOMMY *approaches and helps him up. Helps him on with his coat. He clings to* TOMMY, *who helps him away.*)

59. INT. THE MARTIN HOUSE. NIGHT

Andy's bedroom. LORNA *starts to cry. Tears course down her cheeks.*